Gay Dad

Ten true stories of divorced gay men with kids, living in the UK today.

David Ledain

This edition published in Great Britain 2016
Copyright © David Ledain 2016
David Ledain has asserted his right under the Copyright, Design and Patents Act 1988 to be identified as the author of this book.
All rights reserved. No part of this publication may be reproduced, stored in a retrieval system, or transmitted in any form or by any means, electronic, mechanical, photocopying, recording or otherwise, without the prior permission of the copyright owner.

ISBN-13:978-1530636662

For ALL gay dads everywhere.

Contents

Foreword by Charlie Condou	7
Introduction	11
What do the statistics say?	19
How many gay men end up marrying women?	19
National statistics	19
Do gay men outnumber gay women?	24
Gay city enclaves	25
Does your age help?	26
How gay are you?	28
Adam's Story	34
The UK law on divorce	47
Bert's Story	49
Clause 28	65
Sex and pornography	66
Porn by Alistair Appleton	70
Porn addiction	74
The signs or symptoms of porn addiction	76
What causes porn addiction?	78
How to stop porn addiction	80
Chris' Story	82
Homosexuality & Religion	99
Judaism	99
Christianity	100
The Roman Catholic Church	102
Islam	103
Hinduism	104
Buddhism	105
Sikhism	107
Deep's Story	109
Anti-gay countries of the world	121
Edward's Story	125
Fred's Story	131
Criminal law	149
Cottages/cottaging	151

Grant's Story	156
Harry's Story	162
Where did the term homosexual originate?	167
Ian's Story	174
Gays in ancient cultures	210
Ancient Egypt	214
Ancient Greece	216
Romans	218
Native Americans	220
Imperial China	221
Imperial Japan	225
Mediaeval Europe	228
John's Story	232
Gay slang	239
List of current gay slang words & terminology	246
Polari	256
Helpful links	258
Acknowledgements	262

Foreword by Charlie Condou

Ex-*Coronation Street* actor Charlie Condou, who played midwife Marcus Dent, kindly agreed to provide a foreword for *Gay Dad*. Condou lives with his Canadian husband, Cameron Laux, and his daughter and son, who split their time between Condou and their mother, the actress Catherine Kanter.

When I was approached by David Ledain to write a foreword to his new book, I was unprepared for what I read, for my own story of being a gay father is quite unlike the ones here. I always knew I wanted kids, and I always knew that I was gay and that fatherhood, should I be lucky enough to experience it, would happen to me as a gay man.

I met the mother of my children through my work as an actor, and over many years, we talked about the possibility of having children together. Then I met Cam, my now husband, and the three of us embarked on this co-parenting journey together. Our family life has always been open and public, and it is hard for me to imagine it any other way.

The stories in *Gay Dad* are quite different to mine. They come from men who for family, cultural or religious reasons felt unable to live openly as gay men. Instead they entered into marriages and raised children until the pressure of hiding such an important part of themselves became too much, forcing them out of the closet and into much more open and honest lives.

One of the most striking things about all these stories is how unfounded most of the men's fears were. Over and over we read of wives that accepted, children happily assimilated into new gay relationships, and friends who remain judgement free. These stories are filled with hope.

It is perhaps a sign of the age and country we live in, that as the laws on marriage, age of consent, family life and adoption are finally equalised, and the stigma around homosexuality drops away, the parenting stories of gay men are increasingly like mine. For young gay men coming out today, there are plenty of examples of same-sex parenting. Their role models are no longer confined to the screamingly camp stereotypes of Larry Grayson and John Inman. They can point to gay sportsmen, politicians, scientists, actors and, yes, camp TV hosts. Finally, it feels like we are able to embrace anything and everything about what it means to be gay. We are able to plan lives and families while being true to ourselves.

But the stories here are not just important as pieces of social history, snapshots of gay life in late twentieth-century Britain. Gay culture in twenty-first century Britain may have smashed through barriers like never before, but around the world that is not the case. There are many places and cultures where being gay is still a shock, a crime or, worse, even a death sentence. In those places many gay men will continue to do whatever they need to do to fit in and conform. Many will marry and become fathers, and while parenthood remains one of life's joys, it is tempered with the sadness, shame and fear of having to live lives that are inauthentic.

Gay Dad paints a picture of a changing world. Gay men born into one time and coming out in a more tolerant one. I hope one day that change will be repeated everywhere. The right to a family life is considered one of the principal human rights – something that should be available to all, regardless of sexuality. These stories offer us inspiration that change is not just possible, it is wonderful.

Charlie Condou, March 2016

Introduction

When I first thought about this book, my idea was simply to bring together a group of gay dads and give them the opportunity to tell their stories. I knew from looking for reading material myself that there was very little available for or about gay dads, and nothing at all that spoke to me. What I wanted was a book that would tell me what it was like for other ordinary dads in the same situation, who were coming to terms with what it means to be gay, married with kids and living in modern Britain today.

I had noted the appearance of books by gay celebrities and sports stars who had written about their lives, and one or two 'self-help' genre books written by authors about gay dads in America, which were often about adoption and gay parenting, but there was nothing, as far as I could tell, that represented or was about men like me, who had experienced what I had or lived where I lived, in a society I understood.

I also wanted a book to refer to that gave me some answers to the questions of what it means – this 'homosexual' thing. Why I am this way inclined? How large is this minority I appear to be part of? What does the UK law say about it, and how does it affect divorce matters?

Has homosexuality always existed, and if so, why? How do other cultures view it, and what do the mainstream religions say about it? Where do words such as 'gay' come from? So many questions that I didn't have the solutions or answers to, but through research have discovered and put in this book.

When I started getting in contact with guys whom I thought might be receptive to the idea of setting down their personal stories for a wider audience to read, I didn't quite know what to expect. I certainly hadn't imagined that the stories of these gay men, who found themselves, like me, living their lives within heterosexual marriages, would come from such a wide and differing group. Not only were their social and demographic backgrounds different, but also their religions, their ages, their interests. It might seem obvious to someone on the outside, but when you think you are quite literally the only one, it is difficult to appreciate that indeed, we do come from all walks of life and all of us have amazing individual stories to tell. Some are heartbreakingly difficult, some are positive, most are struggles that have taken years to work through and often with outside help from prescribed antidepressants and counsellors. But walk into any town centre and randomly pick a group of men from the crowds passing by and you would gather just such an eclectic mix – a navy officer, a businessman, a Sikh, a Christian, some of no particular faith; men from strong family backgrounds, others from difficult ones; city-dwellers and those from small villages and towns. These ten men represent a kaleidoscope of family miscellany, career and wealth, and they have come together in this book in a way they probably would never have done so otherwise, each with a unique life story and one shared commonality – that they are gay and have had to wrestle half their lives living in a predominantly heterosexual world.

Of course I had heard of gay men that sometimes did marry women, but I thought that was such a tiny minority, that I was so completely unusual, that if there were others like me out there, I would never find them. I felt I was an outcast, part of no 'gang'. All I knew for sure about myself was that I was not 'gay' in the conventional view of what that meant or what I understood it to mean. I fitted more easily into a 'heterosexual' or superficially 'bisexual' existence, and I say this not simply because it was an easier option, but from the perspective of my character and make-up. Although, had that pressure to conform not been so prevalent, and had my choices been wider and more varied, and had there been any role models

I could have looked up to, other than David Bowie, who knows how my life might have turned out?

Back then (I got married in 1990), the idea of two men marrying and having kids together was absolutely absurd. It didn't ever cross my mind as an option that would ever apply to me or in my lifetime.

It wasn't until my wife and I separated that I started to tentatively put the feelers out to try to connect with other gay men. I hadn't a clue then that there were so many others in exactly the same situation as me, until I discovered a whole group online. They too had fallen in love with a woman and got married against all their natural instincts. Though none of us were forced into the situation, we just didn't listen to what our brains were telling us. Instead, we fought with the inner turmoil that buried everything so deeply, that it was possible to believe that things would be fine. So at last I could talk to other men who knew how I felt, who had gone through the same trauma, who had been lost and were now finding their way. I had found a 'gang' I could belong to at last.

I realised how lucky I was to have stumbled across this group, and I also quickly realised that I had to write that book that I had looked for but couldn't find. I asked them if they would be willing to talk about their experiences, in the hope that it might inspire and encourage other gay dads to realise that they are not alone, that their situations, however they might feel this is not the case, have been repeated up and down the country thousands and thousands of times before, and no doubt have been since the institution of marriage was first set up.

I think gay men in heterosexual relationships, including marriage, is far more normal than any of us imagine. We are fortunate in that we live in a culture today where homosexuality is, by and large, accepted. Of course, this has not always been the case and is indeed only a very recent move forward in our society. It wasn't until the Sexual Offences Act of 1967 that the previously unlawful act of sex between two men was relinquished, but then only between men of twenty-one years of age or over. It took another twenty-seven years before the age was reduced in 1994 to eighteen, and as recently as 2000 and 2003 respectively for the law to reduce the age of consent further to sixteen, the same as for heterosexuals, and to make acts of gross indecency and buggery, and sexual activity between more than two men no longer a crime in the whole of the UK. Still, in many countries of the world, our relaxed laws and liberal attitudes are not held up as virtues of humanity and equality at all.

Even here, some people are still quick to criticise and condemn, and often ask the question 'how could you marry, knowing your sexuality?' It is a question we all ask ourselves, but one thing I can confirm, none of us went into it lightly. We married because we were in love. It seems so simple, and yet it is so true. 'You must be bisexual then,' other people, mostly women, are even quicker to point out, as if putting a label on it somehow makes sense of it – here is a man who is gay and married, and this is what he looks like and how he acts, he must therefore be bisexual. It helps to allay people's fears. If they can call it something, this mystical, untouchable, unseeable thing, they assume they cannot be affected by it. One thing I have learned throughout this process of meeting and speaking to these men and researching the subject is that sexuality is undefinable a lot of the time. It is as unique to each individual as our personalities are. Perhaps that's how we should define it, in the same way we think of personality – it is not something that can or should be labelled succinctly.

Although I married a woman and before that had girlfriends too, I am not attracted to women sexually in any way. I know that now, yet I spent years pretending and deceiving myself that that was not the case, if I could appreciate the aesthetic curves of someone like Marilyn

Monroe and be able to perform in bed with a woman, then I thought I must be bisexual.

I believe we are all somewhere on a very fluid sexuality spectrum, and I suspect, and I have no evidence for this, that more men probably fall into the bi or bi-curious zone than women. My reasoning is simply that men can perform sexually without there needing to be an emotional connection as well every time. I'm not suggesting that women cannot or do not ever want or crave a rampant session of flesh-on-flesh with someone they are not emotionally tied to, but for men it is all so much easier. We can get up and walk away afterwards, and get on with our lives as if nothing has happened. Women, on the other hand, tend to treat sex as a way of increasing and developing the bond with their partner. For them it's about feelings and sensuality. It can be for men too, of course, but I think we find it a more straightforward process to differentiate between sex for what it is, and making love. I'm no sexologist or psychologist, but having lived and shared a bed with a woman for many years, I base my opinions on having been in both camps, as it were. The sooner it becomes so 'normal' for people to live with whichever adult sexual partner they wish without people batting an eyelid, the better, but until that moment arrives, we have to keep putting the word out there, and I hope this book will go some way to express the normalcy of 'sexuality'.

The stories of these ten men are presented in no particular order and are meant to convey nothing but that which each of the men have written themselves. I have changed their names, places and other factual identifiers to keep their identities anonymous, although some of the men were more than happy to have their names printed, but for the sake of everyone, I have not done so.

With regards to the writing, these men are not writers or authors, they are simply telling their stories. I have taken the liberty of tidying up here and there, but other than that, these are their words in every sense. The moral of this collection of stories is how very similar they all are in their emotional struggles and determination always to do what is right. Each is a vignette of life as lived by them, but shared by so many others, and here we can open the front door of many a modern home in Britain today and take a peek inside.

What do the statistics say?

How many gay men end up marrying women?

A conservative figure often quoted on the Internet estimates that in the US there are roughly two million lesbian, gay, bisexual, and transgender individuals who have married someone of the opposite sex. Of a total population in the United States of 318,900,000, this figure of two million represents 0.63 per cent. If we applied the same percentage ruling to the 2011 UK census population of 48,085,000 adults aged twenty and over, we get to a figure of 302,935, which would equate to approximately 1 in every 158 UK adults (20+) being LGBT and having been married to someone of the opposite sex, which seems a somewhat high figure. Or is it?

National Statistics

The Integrated Household Survey, published by the Office for National Statistics (ONS), provides the following estimates for the adult UK population in 2011. The numbers which include gender, location and age might appear surprising, but the ONS asked 178,197 people about their sexual identity.

- 1.1 per cent – (1,960) approximately 528,935 adults 20+ of the total population at the time of the survey, identify as gay or lesbian

- 0.4 per cent – (713) approximately 192,340 total pop. adults identify as bisexual

- 0.3 per cent – (535) approximately 144,255 total pop. adults identify as 'other'

- 3.6 per cent – (6,415) approximately 1,731,060 total pop. adults replied 'don't know' or refused to answer the question

- 0.6 per cent – (1,069) approximately 288,510 total pop. adults provided 'no response' to the question

- 2.7 per cent – 204,962 of 16 to 24-year-olds of a population of just over 7.5million in the UK in 2011, identify themselves as gay, lesbian or bisexual

- this compares to 0.4 per cent – 41,600 of 65 years + out of a population of 10,400,000 in the UK in 2011, who also identify themselves as gay, lesbian or bisexual

From these statistics, we can gather that approximately 1 in every 100 people in Britain will identify themselves as gay, bisexual or lesbian. Other sources provide alternative estimates of the sexual orientation of the population. The British Journal of Psychiatry published in 2004, estimated that it was nearer 5 per cent (2.6 million) of the British population that was gay, whereas another government figure in 2005 estimated that there were 3.6 million (6 per cent). Though this was questioned in a report by the Equality and Human Rights Commission, which described that figure as debateable when set against other available survey estimates.

Other figures range from one in five or, as many believe it to be, nearer one in ten. The number 'one in ten' has long been recognised in popular culture as a reliable guesstimate on homosexuality in the population. This idea made its way into the public consciousness through press coverage on the two books known as the Kinsey Reports, *Sexual Behaviour in the Human Male* (written in 1948) and *Sexual Behaviour in the Human Female* (1953), by American zoologist Alfred Kinsey, in which he claimed 10 per cent of the US population were gay, lesbian or bisexual.

Though the reports broke long-held taboos on reporting about sexual orientation, the methodology used by Kinsey quickly came in for criticism for being extremely unreliable. Soon after it was published, statisticians from the American Statistical Association claimed 'a random selection of three people would have been better than a group of three hundred chosen by Kinsey'. Some people think the number might be even higher than Kinsey suggested. In 2011, when a Gallup poll asked over 1,000 US adults, 'What percentage of Americans today would you say are gay or lesbian?' the resulting answer was that, on average, respondents guessed 1 in 4 Americans were. A quarter of the population? This seems ludicrously high and begs the question whether this is how Americans perceive their fellow citizens or if it is a statement about how 'gay' they see their society becoming?

The UK Treasury came up with their estimate when analysing the financial implications of the new Civil Partnerships Act (2004), allowing same-sex partners to marry and which gives them similar rights as heterosexual married couples in areas such as tax, pensions and inheritance.

Stonewall, the gay rights charity, thought the number of LGBT people in the population was closer to between 5% and 7%, which they thought was a 'reasonable estimate'.

According to the Department of Trade and Industry, they estimate there are 1.5 to 2 million gay men, lesbians and bisexuals in the 30-million-strong UK workforce. Given the UK population of 64 million, this would mean the gay community is between 4 and 5 million people. Publication of such figures has encouraged big-name companies to join the growing rush to cash in on the potential of the gay economy, or the 'pink pound' as it has become known. One research showed that gays and lesbians could be enjoying a combined annual income of £60 billion, and among the respondents to this particular survey, 40 per cent of the women and 25 per cent of the men were professionals; 11 per cent of women and 13 per cent of men were managers; 5 per cent of women and 6 per cent of men were senior managers; and 8 per cent of both sexes were clerical and office workers.

It can appear to be all very confusing, and as someone who has worked in market research, I know how easy it is to come up with two conflicting conclusions by pulling numbers from the same data and interpreting or presenting them differently. What we need, as our society is becoming more open to gay community needs and aspirations, is broader scientifically conducted research. We also need to understand the reasons 3.6 per cent of people in the ONS survey replied 'don't know' to the question of their sexuality, 0.3 per cent said 'other', and most importantly, why 0.6 per cent refused to answer the question at all.

Commercially, trying to target a marketing campaign at an audience, a significant number of whom remain closeted and hidden, is very difficult. To date, the only real beneficiaries of this huge marketplace are Internet porn channels and dating sites. Government and businesses, big and small, need to lead in this respect. Increasingly, we are starting to see male couples portrayed in positive situations in advertising, and the more the gay community responds to the pull of favourable adverts by dipping into their pockets, the more commonplace such images will become. A note to the business world: We need to be coaxed and seduced, and we need to feel safe.

Do gay men outnumber gay women?

While 1.5 per cent of men in the UK say they are gay, only 0.7 per cent of women say the same. That is reversed, however, when it comes to identifying as 'bisexual'; 0.3 per cent of men select this, compared to 0.5 per cent of women. Slightly more women (3.8%) than men (3.5%) 'don't know' or refuse to answer the question. I would suggest that we have to take into account a certain amount of British reserve in answering questions on sexuality, even if it is carried out anonymously. Paper surveys are liable to be read by any member of the household, but it would be interesting to understand how such households in the 'don't knows' and especially the 'refusers', are made up – whether there are children, spouses or other individuals living with the responders.

It also opens the debate about the whole concept of homosexuality versus bisexuality, and gay men and women's perceptions of those 'roles'. I believe men are more inclined to be gay than women, and it would seem the 0.8 per cent difference between men identifying as gay and women who do so bears this out. Women, it appears, are also more likely to swing both ways.

Gay city enclaves

Not unsurprisingly, the percentage of British people saying they're gay, lesbian or bisexual is far higher in London than anywhere else in the UK – 2.5 per cent compared to just 1.1 per cent in Northern Ireland and 1 per cent in the East of England. Very often, minorities 'levitate' towards areas where they feel safest and among their own. Most capital cities in Europe have districts that cater to the artistic, avant-garde, gay crowd.

Brighton in the UK has had a long LGBT history and association since the nineteenth century when many men were drawn there by the large concentration of soldiers garrisoned in the town during the Napoleonic Wars. Evidence suggests the transient population and good transport links with London helped in its reputation as a place for homosexuals to come and enjoy time by the seaside and to be at ease amongst their own. By the 1930s, Brighton started to flourish as the biggest gay destination outside London, and many gay pubs and clubs started to establish themselves. During the Second World War, Brighton was again full of servicemen away from home, meeting gay people for the first time, and this helped boost Brighton's reputation for its special pleasures and helped to grow it into today's 'gay capital' of the UK.

Does your age help?

According to the ONS survey, 2.7 per cent of those aged between 16 and 24 said they were gay, lesbian or bisexual. The percentage went down, the older the respondents – 2.1 per cent of 25-to-34-year-olds, 1.9 per cent of 35-to-49-year-olds, 1.0 per cent of 50-to-64-year-olds, and 0.5 per cent of 65+ years. Clearly it is easier for younger people these days to declare their sexuality than it was for the older generations in their times, and one can assume a certain amount of reticence on their part about divulging such personal information, but does it actually mean that there are less homosexual people in the higher age groups? This breakdown of responders to this ONS survey might imply the extent to which taboos over sexuality still persist, particularly for older people and those living in more conservative parts of the country, yet maybe for optimistic, utopian reasons or indeed concerns over the abundance and seeming proliferation of 'gayness' in society today, they might therefore overestimate the number of gay people they perceive to be living amongst us – one in four versus one in ten.

How gay are you?

My feeling is probably less than one in ten people are gay, but more than we think. One in ten would mean that at least two people at my old workplace were homosexuals. I was one, but who was the other? The very question about one's sexuality is so idiosyncratic it is difficult to know how any such straw polls can be taken of the whole population, but there must be a better way than asking simply if someone is straight, gay or bisexual. A truthful and reliable picture of how the country's population is made up would make good economic sense both for the gay community and government alike.

Perhaps the question of whether you identify as gay, straight or bisexual is better asked with a scale of gayness attached to it: one being totally straight and ten, totally gay, many people would place themselves somewhere along that scale, but fewer would put themselves at the number one or number ten spots. Even the halfway point at number five, i.e., exactly half and half and totally bisexual, seems to be too restricting. Sexual preference and desire often depends on much more than simply the sex of the person in question. Given the option of two equally gorgeous individuals to sleep with, one male and one female, I would choose the guy, but that is too simplistic. A bisexual man might also choose the good-looking young man over the voluptuous young woman, but does that make him more gay?

The Kinsey scale (as invented by Alfred Kinsey in 1948) ranges from 0, for those who would identify themselves as exclusively heterosexual with no experience with or desire for sexual activity with someone of the same sex, to 6, for those who would identify themselves as exclusively homosexual with no experience with or desire for sexual activity with those of the opposite sex, and 1-5 for those who would identify themselves with varying levels of desire for sexual activity with either sex, including incidental or occasional desire for sexual activity with the same sex.

Rating/Description

- 0 Exclusively heterosexual
- 1 Predominantly heterosexual, only incidentally homosexual
- 2 Predominantly heterosexual, but more than incidentally homosexual
- 3 Equally heterosexual and homosexual
- 4 Predominantly homosexual, but more than incidentally heterosexual

- 5 Predominantly homosexual, only incidentally heterosexual
- 6 Exclusively homosexual
- X No socio-sexual contacts or reactions

It is interesting to note also that Kinsey believed that sexual preference changed with age which implies there is much more to sexuality than a single gene. According to Kinsey's reports, 11.6 per cent of white males aged 20 to 35 years were given a rating of 3 for that period of their lives, and 10 per cent of American males surveyed were 'more or less exclusively homosexual for at least three years between the ages of 16 and 55' (i.e. in the 5 to 6 range). So the magical figure of ten per cent is by no means static and can vary dependent on the age bracket being looked at.

Try the Kinsey scale for yourself here: http://vistriai.com/kinseyscaletest/

There are now new ways of measuring sexuality that include even more options than the Kinsey scale.

THE
PURPLE-RED
SCALE OF ATTRACTION

ORIENTATION

F6	F5	F4	F3	F2	F1	F0
E6	E5	E4	E3	E2	E1	E0
D6	D5	D4	D3	D2	D1	D0
C6	C5	C4	C3	C2	C1	C0
B6	B5	B4	B3	B2	B1	B0
A	A	A	A	A	A	A

ATTRACTION TYPE

ATTRACTION TYPES
- **A (Aromantic Asexuality):** Experiences no attraction, besides friendship and/or aesthetic attraction.
- **B (Romantic Asexuality):** Not interested in sexual relations whatsoever, but open to romance, touch or bonds stronger than friendship/
- **C (Tertiary Sexuality):** Experiences no sexual attraction, but willing to do it for other reasons, such as children, pleasing their partners, etc.
- **D (Secondary Sexuality):** May develop lustful feelings over the course of a relationship, but not at first.
- **E (Primary Sexuality):** Sexual desire is established from the get-go, even if it is not acted upon. However, other components (such as companionship) are essential to these individuals.
- **F (Hyper Sexuality):** Sex is the be-all-end-all purpose of any relationship. Everything else is just a consolation prize or means to an end.

ORIENTATIONS
- **0:** Exclusively attracted to opposite sex.
- **1:** Mostly attracted to the opposite sex.
- **2:** Prefers the opposite sex, but is also attracted to the same sex
- **3:** Equal Attraction (Bisexual or biromantic)
- **4:** Prefers the same sex, but is also attracted to the opposite sex.
- **5:** Mostly attracted to the same sex.
- **6:** Exclusively attracted to the same sex.

The Purple-Red scale measures attraction in two ways. The first measures orientation and remains much the same as the Kinsey scale. The second measures *how* attracted you are to people ranging from A (Aromantic Asexuality), which means you experience no attraction besides friendship, to F (Hyper Sexuality) where sex is the only interest. This new scale has received mixed reviews. Some agree that it definitely improves upon the Kinsey scale, while others have criticised it for melding sex and gender together and that it also implies that romantic attraction is a requirement for sexual attraction.

The problem with the Kinsey scale is that it does not address all possible sexual expressions. There have been studies where the scale used is wider, from 0 to 10, where 0 would be completely gay and 10 completely heterosexual, and the question simply put, 'what is your orientation number?' Others have defined it further. Michael Storms, of the University of Kansas, proposed a two-dimensional map of erotic orientation showing four sexual orientation categories: homosexual, bisexual, asexual and heterosexual. This model addressed several inadequacies with the one-dimensional Kinsey scale. Firstly, the Kinsey scale had no way to distinguish between strong attraction to males and females, and little to no attraction to either males or females. Kinsey also had no way of dealing with asexuals and simply labelled them X, a point off of the scale. By placing hetero- and homo-eroticism on two axes, Storms' model can account for asexuality and more accurately describe bisexuality.

Fritz Klein, in his Klein Sexual Orientation Grid, includes factors such as how orientation can change throughout a person's lifetime, as well as emotional and social orientation. Try it for yourself here:

http://sid.southampton.gov.uk/kb5/southampton/directory/advice.page?id=RsuF5ehfWvQ&familychannel=10-4

Kinsey, Storm, and Klein are only three of more than two hundred different scales that measure and describe sexual orientation. Many sexologists today regard the Kinsey scale as relevant to sexual orientation, but not comprehensive enough to cover all sexual identities. The premise now is that sexual identity involves at least three different spectra, **sexual orientation being only one of them. Biological sex and gender identity** also have a strong causal effect.

This is Adam's Story

Born in the early '60s, the youngest of five, I had three sisters and a brother who came out as gay when I was ten, more of that later.

At fourteen months I had a serious accident at home involving the coal fire and spent the rest of my childhood in and out of a children's burns ward. I think this was very formative, in that I missed out on a lot of the 'normal' experiences of childhood, and instead I mixed with disfigured kids in an institution, where I met my first friend. We spent a couple of weeks innocently sitting in each other's beds.

I grew up a very angry and hurt misfit, and I did not trust my mother. It was normal policy in those days to not distress children by informing them of upcoming hospital visits. I never knew if it was a check-up or a bath-and-pyjamas situation.

My first homoerotic experience was with a bunch of lads rolling down a hill together with our pants around our ankles. The grass tickled. At the age of ten, two important things happened. I got caught experimenting with a friend by the local bullies. We were curious about each other's bodies, and the experience was sensual rather than sexual, but oh dear, the bother it caused in our small community. The second important thing that happened was that my brother, after a few years of rumours, came out to the village then promptly left for college, leaving me to cope with the backlash, and especially with my own reputation, having myself been caught in a compromising situation. If the local kids had access to pitchforks and flaming brands, they would have used them.

I quickly learned to avoid certain places and situations, as in, basically anywhere outside of my home, and spent my teenage years avoiding school in order not have to defend myself. During the day I would often help myself to a bottle of my dad's brown ale and a selection of my mother's many pharmaceuticals and head off into the local woods for an adventure rather than go to school. One of the fathers in my street one day actually stood by while he set his son on me, and often the local gang thought it a laugh to send their new sidekicks over to punch the poof. Even though violence makes me physically sick, I had a lot of anger boiling inside me, and each of these lads only ever bullied me once – being stomped and battered by a queer is very embarrassing.

After leaving school at sixteen and attempting to train as a draughtsman for British Telecom (showing my age there), I enrolled at the local college to study applied design and never missed a day. It opened up my small-village mentality and encouraged me to embrace difference. My tutor often wore eyeshadow and played avant-garde bagpipes before being sectioned. I met some of my best friends there and went on to study fine art and realised that it was almost compulsory to experiment with sexuality and gender identity. Art school saved my life!

I suppose having three older sisters, I have always been able to relate to women on their terms and have had long-term monogamous relationships, and a few brief love affairs with women. When single anything goes, and at art school I was openly bisexual, which I think some women found attractive, and a few men as well. I like having an emotional bond with women, and most of my friends are of the female persuasion, but my most powerful needs and urges are towards men. I have recently learned to proudly state that 'I like cock!'

In the mid-eighties I returned home and played keyboard for local bands and started my career as an archaeologist. I'd only had a flat for a month when this mad, stunningly beautiful woman slept in my spare bedroom after a party. I met her in my favourite haunt when she was pretending to be French with her friend. My first words to her were, *'Tu est l'etoil de la nuit'*, 'You are the star of my night', in my best Geordie accent. Que look of total bafflement! From then on we became best mates and partners-in-crime. We rented properties together, and although a certain amount of bed-hopping went on, we always kept separate rooms to accommodate our current lovers, who we used to vie for, and Ruby was often annoyed that I had got there first. We would make a point of introducing each other to them as 'the future parent of my child'.

In the mid-nineties, the biological clock started its countdown. We decided to commit to each other and concentrated on making a baby, and that came true in 1997. After a few miscarriages, we received the good news. A letter through our door from her doctor demanded a meeting that day, no matter what time it was, even if it was a home visit after hours. Ruby had been ill on and off for some years. Her doctor had been through her notes and taken some blood tests to confirm that she had probably got hepatitis C, since living in Edinburgh in the early eighties, (think *Trainspotting*), and that she probably had less than five years to live.

We sat in bed all that night and talked and cried and talked some more. The medical team were adamant that we have an abortion, as our child would be ill all their life and not live to be twenty. Ruby had chosen me as a sensitive bisexual man, to be the father of her child (she had issues with straight men from her past), and in the early hours of that morning we made a pact, that twenty years of being loved is better than not being born at all. We would stick together, and when the time came, I would take on the responsibility of raising our child no matter what.

The most wonderful person to ever enter my life came into being after a difficult birth, and we had to wait a further nine months for the test results to give him the all-clear, which was a great relief but also marked the period when Ruby entered the late stages of her disease and my life became unbearable.

Most people are unaware of the cognitive damage caused by hep C. I was in my mid-thirties, supervising major excavations at work and returning home of an evening, to cook, tidy, care for a baby boy and deal with the constant repetition and delusions of my best friend, his mother. I learned to be wary of the signs of imminent blackouts and be ready to jump in case she collapsed with, or sometimes onto, our baby. She was constantly covered in bruises and black eyes when she would hit the coffee table or the sink as she blacked out. We had kept her illness a secret, and rumours started to spread, and behind my back I was gaining a reputation as a wife-beater.

As the illness progressed, things got worse, and all the anger and despair had to go somewhere and I was there to receive it. I went to sleep at night scared that I would be woken in the early hours being attacked by the woman I loved, blank-eyed and not remembering a thing the next morning. I kept a sleeping bag hidden in the shed, just in case, and often turned up for work barely able to manage the site, which was noticed by my boss and eventually led to me losing my position at the university.

It all finally unravelled one evening after work when she secretly rang the police before attacking me with a baseball bat while I was holding our son in my arms. After a night in the cells, battered and bruised, it was time to get out. (Legally, in a domestic situation, the man is taken into custody, unless he is willing to press charges against the mother). It broke my heart and triggered a nervous breakdown. I am very grateful to my good friend who took me in and tolerated my post break-up behaviour for the next year – I gave him a water pistol to shoot me when I was wallowing in it.

In 2001 I moved back to my hometown and dropped all contact with everybody except trusted friends, (anybody wishing to contact me had to phone my mother first to be vetted). I was very much not welcomed and received threats should I be seen in certain pubs and clubs, and the only thing that kept me out of hospital was the fact that I cared for my son. They blamed me for Ruby's physical and mental decline.

By this time, Ruby, who was both my best friend and worst enemy, had become very erratic and social services had become involved. It was time to commit to my promise, and our son came to live with me before he was taken into care as being 'at risk'. The next thing I knew, I was the bastard who had taken Ruby's son away from her – and this was from the hypocrites who contacted social services in the first place.

Later that year Ruby decided she was well enough to care for our son with the support of her family, and I reluctantly agreed to a trial period, even though I begged her not to, as I knew the stress would trigger a crisis for her. Within a month she had collapsed with a brain haemorrhage and after major surgery was left unable to speak, crippled down one side and subject to epileptic fits. Our son moved back with me, his dad, and had supervised visits to his mother.

In 2007, just when it looked like Ruby was stable and able to live an independent life, I received a phone call: she had collapsed at home and hit her head on the corner of a radiator. I had to identify her body, which had lain there, being slowly cooked, for three days. I can still see her when I close my eyes, and I told the police officer that he would not believe she had once been so stunningly beautiful.

Being a single man raising a child in a traditional working-class area is not a laugh. Standing alone in the playground, kiddie's parties and junior league football matches, never quite trusted or understood, possibly even a threat to the other mothers' positions as providers and carers – if this man can do it, then perhaps their estranged husbands could as well? The men were just disturbed that I had taken on a 'feminine role'. On top of that, they presumed that because I have a son, I am straight. Taking on the role of both parents is a bit strange to their way of thinking; a child should be with his mother, full stop.

Eventually, my friend and godfather to my son noticed how much stress I was under, and it was time to tell the truth to my son, as he was getting older, and someday soon someone would make a comment that would lead him to realise that his dad is gay. My friend was right in saying that I had a responsibility to tell my son the truth before he found out from others.

The three of us sat down one evening and I told my son my truth; his godfather sat and mediated, explaining things as a straight man and also as a friend of his dad's. There were a lot of tears, and my son was quiet and withdrawn for a few days afterwards, but things settled down once he realised that nothing had changed apart from the fact that his dad loved him enough to be totally honest with him about a very painful subject. This was the beginning of my coming out. Once I had done that most difficult thing, the rest was easy. My son's main concern was that he would be bullied and excluded if it became known that his dad was gay. So my coming out had to be gradual and natural, on a trust and need-to-know basis, and he has done the same with his friends at school, who think it's 'cool'. Last year he told me it was time for me to start finding a life of my own, as he was old enough now for me to be independent from him – cheeky lad. He encouraged me to get involved in the local gay rugby team – though he takes the micky about me socialising with a bunch of burly sweaty blokes.

John is now seventeen, doing well at school, has a part-time job at a local music and arts venue, and is about to start driving lessons. He has his mother's looks and his dad's attitude. He is clever, funny and wiser than his years. It's been such a painful journey, but it has led to where I am now, and I would not change a thing.

Some of Adam's Internet posts of his 'everyday life'.

'The only problem is that everyone has to be informed of my status as a "GAY" man.'

'Last weekend I had a local on my doorstep "kicking-off" because I was too friendly and therefore obviously shagging his girlfriend, and then one of my neighbours commented "but he's GAY!" I am sure we all know the silence that follows that statement and, I have to say, the embarrassment we have to deal with at that moment.'

'The best comment is "Are you, because I don't mind if you are", to which I remind them that I don't care if they mind because I don't care whether they care. It's not that important.'

'Everybody presumes that because I have a teenage son, I am therefore straight.'

'I have to say that the ex-prison "blokes" of a certain age are willing to talk to me about this, although

they think that gay sex outside is another matter and not to be spoken of unless you're having a good time.'

'It's a twice-a-year thing and it bores me.'

'Again another fit and furry bloke with a lovely accent and a passion for beer and rugby moves into the area and gravitates "straight" for me as a friend – loads of manly hugs and "proper" hand-shakes and compliments about my age and looks (Bastard! I'm only fifty-three).'

'After the last "misunderstanding" with the gorgeous and ginger Malcolm frae Scotland, I decided to stop getting involved with hetty blokes. Malcolm continues to be a friend and good neighbour after a drunken night of man stuff, which he regretted the next day, but an understanding and a handshake sorted that.'

'Finished work and called into the local shop/community centre/gossip factory that is directly opposite my flat, to find myself in a very prolonged conversation and the manly embrace of Dan (early thirties, size and build of a prop and hazel brown eyes + that accent and attitude of an excited puppy) – had to drag myself out and away from him in the hope that the rest of the customers/neighbours might explain that even though I have a teenage son, like rugby and have a lot of female

friends, it does not mean that I am straight; two out of three is a bit of a giveaway.'

'I admit that I "act straight" because from my point of view, I act like myself. I am just a gay Geordie bloke with a kid to care for, and I appear to be exactly who I am, and why should I have to constantly "out myself" to other people for their sake.'

'When I came out to John, I promised him that I would not make a scene or be the conventional idea of a Gay Man (definitely not that).'

'The truth will out and over the years most of my community has realised that having a son does not require me to be straight. It's been an organic thing of rumours, shock and acceptance.'

'It's about to become the time where my son will have to confront his Gay Dad situation with the rest of the school and his ex-football crowd – just in time for his exams.'

'Please bear in mind that we live in a very narrow-minded and blinkered backwoods of society, and we are not talking about barely sentient pond scum.'

'I am sure that he may have discussed me with his closest friends, (I do dress eccentrically!) but may not want that sort of public attention during his exam year.'

'He spent his Primary School years with people trying to bully him about his unusual dad and dead mother; although he has learnt to shrug things off and brave-face things, I have no idea how he will deal with this situation. We both knew that it would happen when I first explained myself to him. That was his major concern at the time.'

'To be honest, this will happen anyway as a consequence of my being myself, and he is now sixteen with a couple of broken-hearted girlfriends behind him and a bunch of the usual unpopular friends who question the conventions. They all think that his dad is chilled and sorted, so there is hope for the future yet.'

The UK law on divorce

When a woman contacted her lawyer to obtain a divorce from her husband because he was gay, she assumed there would be two grounds for divorce open to her – adultery or unreasonable behaviour. Instead, she was surprised to find that adultery was not an option, because her husband had sex with other men and not other women. In the UK, adultery can only occur between members of the opposite sex and must involve vaginal intercourse. Case law defines adultery as 'voluntary sexual intercourse between a man and a woman who are not married to each other but one or both of whom is or are married,' says Jonathan West, head of family and marriage law at Prolegal.

For divorce proceedings to go through when one partner in the marriage is gay, adultery cannot, therefore, be cited. There are five grounds for a divorce in England and Wales – adultery, unreasonable behaviour, desertion, having lived apart for more than two years (if both partners agree to divorce), or having lived apart for more than five years (if only one wishes to divorce).

This differs in Scotland and Northern Ireland, but in all parts of the UK, adultery is defined in the same way, and divorce law stipulates that you must show there are good reasons for ending a marriage. So if there are no grounds for adultery in a marriage ending due to homosexual acts, unreasonable behaviour is the obvious alternative, but it is important to be mindful that the UK courts in regard to divorce law do not give a jot about whether one of the parties in the marriage has committed an adulterous act or not, even a gay one, when they are asked to decide on matters relating either to the financial arrangements or the children. The fact of 'adultery' or 'unreasonable behaviour' because of homosexual relations outside the marriage is irrelevant to these decisions, and the days when the courts 'punished' someone for such things have long gone.

Do seek legal advice. More often than not, the sticking point in any divorce settlement is the splitting of assets between the two parties. Most solicitors will urge their clients to fight for every penny, but if you still have an amicable relationship, it is far better to try to sort these things out between you both. Sometimes it might take a letter from your solicitors to ensure the other side does not take advantage, but once you are reasonably happy with your outcome, don't try to grab more.

This is Bert's Story

Like most people, I have numerous scattered and patchy memories of events and people from my very young childhood, but the one thing I don't remember is at what point I first realised I preferred boys to girls. I'm pretty sure I always did, and it's something I think my parents realised, or at least suspected, throughout my pre-adult years, but which was naturally never talked about. I didn't like sport, I still don't, I was very shy around girls; hell, my parents even had photos of me playing with dolls at the age of three or four. So I guess the signs were always there.

One thing I do remember quite vividly is at around the age of eight some of my fellow Cub Scouts teased me relentlessly for hanging around with the more effeminate boys, the 'poofy' or 'sissy' boys, as they referred to them. It was also at this age that I first heard a little ditty that went:

'It's a fella's occupation,
to stick his cockilation,
in a woman's ventilation,
to increase the population,
of the younger generation.'

When the meaning of it was explained to me, I was mortified to think that someone of the opposite sex was going to *see* my willy, let alone what I was expected to do with it. Of course, social and peer pressure and parental expectations resulted in me eventually doing just what the limerick said I should do.

My teens were an agonising and confusing period, just like most pubescent boys, I should think. I had a crush on the hunky games teacher and had difficulty knowing where to look in the showers, particularly when the athletic boys with their well-developed cocks and sprouting pubes stood there with everything hanging out, large and glorious, for all to see. Those very same boys and the games teacher were often in my wet dreams of a night. Thankfully I was never bullied at school, but the popular and 'with it' boys seemed to know somehow and openly sniggered at me.

To add to my confusion, I didn't know what or who I was. Of course I knew who I was from the point of my family and parentage, but I wasn't aware of anyone else who was gay, and therefore, I couldn't identify or define myself as that. The only point of reference I had was television characters like Mr Humphreys from *Are You Being Served?*, Larry Grayson, and 'Honky Tonk' from the *Dick Emery Show*, and I knew I wasn't like any of them, nor did I want to be. Consequently, I had this internal struggle between who I really was, or my desires, and just wanting to fit in – wanting to be like everyone else. Wanting to be normal.

That said, at around the age of sixteen I did find myself 'experimenting' on a few occasions with a couple of my mates. Once in a tent in my parents' back garden, with a lad from up the road, which led both to the receiving and giving of my first blow job (I quickly realised I liked both). This was followed a couple of months later with the same lad in my bedroom while my parents slept in the next room. Thinking about it now, I come out in a cold sweat, appreciating how easy it would have been for us to have been caught, but I guess at the time, the risk of that was all part of the excitement. Another occasion was with my best friend's brother, who although only six months younger than me, was a whole school year below. We found ourselves, one afternoon, giving each other massages, which eventually resulted in my thumbs working their way beneath the waistband of his underpants and brushing the helmet of his almost fully erect cock. Whilst we were both clearly aroused by this, I was concerned that he might have jumped up at any minute and asked, 'What the f### do you think you're doing?' but he didn't, and in fact, we ended up wrestling and trying to insert ice cubes between each other's arse cheeks. We have remained friends ever since, but needless to say, the events of that afternoon have never been talked about or repeated.

By the time I'd reached the age of eighteen, I'd only had one girlfriend and questions were beginning to be asked, and not just behind my back either. So I jumped at the chance when my ice-cube mate asked if I would double date with him and his girlfriend on New Year's Eve. By all accounts, his girlfriend wasn't prepared to go out and celebrate without taking her best friend along with her, so a solution had to be found, and the answer was to include me. The evening was fun, and the girl and I seemed to get on well, so I plucked up courage and asked her on another date without the other two. Following that second date, I introduced her to my parents, and it was on this occasion that it became apparent to me what they had been thinking throughout my childhood, as my mother, bless her soul, announced how pleased they both were to meet my girlfriend, as they were convinced I was going to grow up a poof. Well, you can imagine my shock at this revelation, and rather than this be a catalyst for me to be who I truly was, it just strengthened my resolve to be normal, to fit in and fulfil my parents' now clear expectations of me.

I suppose we, or rather I, went through the motions of being boyfriend and girlfriend, particularly as I enjoyed the normality of it and the fact that it masked the other thoughts going through my head. Nevertheless, it didn't stop the sneaky looks at attractive guys, nor the fantasies I had, both on my own and during our hetero sex.

You have to remember, I was born in the sixties, at a time when homosexuality was illegal, and I grew up with the generation above me having that narrow frame of mind and opinion. There was no Internet and the pornographic laws of the seventies and eighties meant you had very little, shall we say, research material to hand. When I was of an age to discover my body and the pleasures of a good handjob, the papers and news reports were full of stories about AIDS – the Gay Plague, as it was dubbed. Needless to say, this scared the hell out of a confused gay lad in his mid-teens, and by the time I'd reached eighteen and wanted to find out more about my feelings and thoughts, Clause 28* had raised its ugly head and come into existence.

The stress and pressure of coming to terms with who I was and the more than likely disappointment of my parents, not to mention the fear of ridicule by my peers and the animosity of society in general, was overwhelming to me. So somehow I settled things in my mind and decided that a normal life, a life like that of my parents, aunts and uncles and the parents of all my friends, together with the strong wish to have children of my own, outweighed my desire to follow my true path in life.

I persisted with the charade of being a boyfriend for a total of seven years. We lived together in our own little house with a mortgage over our heads and even got engaged, though we never set a date. For some reason something was holding us both back. In fact, for twelve months or so we lived more like brother and sister, and there had been no sexual activity between us during this final period, so we both decided to end it. In truth, I had lost any sexual desire, as I had started to think more about the life I could have led, rather than the one I was living, and I was clearly not happy with how I was feeling. Yet, I was still not courageous enough to say 'you know what, I'm a gay guy, get over it', but rather convinced myself that I was probably bisexual and had chosen to live a straight man's life rather than that of a gay man.

My life up until this point had been about denying who I was, so I hadn't had any real experience of being gay. I'd not been to any gay bars or nightclubs. How could I, when I didn't even know where they were? I hadn't had any real sexual experiences and I hadn't even kissed a guy properly and I was now twenty-five years old. That all could have changed if I'd held my nerve with what eventually happened sometime in December 1992.

There had been the odd occasion in the years between being sixteen and twenty-five when I'd been touched up in a busy pub or nightclub, or propositioned by an older guy, and even had my head turned by the goings on in the local woods, but I had brushed all this aside purely because of the fear of being discovered and the embarrassment that would have caused me. In December 1992 I was twenty-six and at the office Christmas party. Rob, a suspected gay guy in the office, walked up to me and gave me a full-on passionate kiss, and do you know what, whilst I enjoyed every second of it and found myself becoming aroused, fear and embarrassment struck again, and I took flight, straight out of the bar and on to the first train home. For the benefit of my work colleagues I laughed the whole thing off the following Monday morning, ensuring the end of anything with Rob before it had even begun. I was a fool, and at times I often think I still am.

Six months later I moved from the north, where I'd grown up and lived until just after my twenty-seventh birthday, and moved south. The perfect time to start all over again and be who I really was, you would think, but by now being 'normal' had become ingrained in me, and the wish to make my parents proud was still all-consuming. I had at least decided one thing, that what will be, will be, and I had concluded that if I ended up single and unmarried for the rest of my life, so be it. Stupidly I still didn't have the courage or strength of character to seek out those people I know today make me feel accepted and comfortable with who I am – in a word 'complete', even though at the time I was working with a couple of out and proud gay guys.

When I met my wife eighteen months later, I genuinely wanted to be with her and marry her. I had fallen in love with her almost from day one. In my mind I had decided this was the woman I would spend the remainder of my life with, the woman with whom I would have a family, so I accepted that all the other thoughts I'd had for all those years would be pushed into the far recesses of my mind and just be fantasies. That is how things were for the next twelve years or so.

We got married in the spring of 1996, a couple of months before I turned thirty, and the children started arriving two years later. Around 2003 we had cable TV installed, and because I sometimes had to work from home, we soon followed this up with broadband. Having broadband now meant we could have a PC, and thus came my discovery of gay porn.

I now had an outlet for my sexual frustrations brought about by all those thoughts I was constantly banishing to the dark recesses of my mind. So when the kids were in bed and my wife was out with friends, I would steal away and log on to various gay porn sites and relieve myself of those frustrations. I'd started with soft-core, but quickly worked my way up to hard-core gay porn movies. Now as anyone with an addiction knows, you start to take risks, and I was no exception. I started to log on when the kids were not yet asleep, or when my wife was only nipping out to the shops, and inevitably there were an increasing number of close shaves.

Generally, I would say I was content with my life at the time, but I wasn't truly happy. We seemed to be existing as a family rather than living. A significant change, however, came less than a month after my fortieth birthday, when, sadly, my mother suddenly passed away. She was only sixty, and I think I subconsciously realised the shortness and fragility of life. I started to reassess my own life, and whilst I had no regrets about the things I had done, I did regret the things I hadn't.

Following the death of my mother, a couple of other significant events took place over the next eighteen months to two years that tested the foundations of our marriage, and although we seemed to survive these, I think the countdown to our separation, four years later, had begun.

I mentioned earlier that if you have an addiction, you have a tendency to take risks, and by my early to mid-forties, gay porn had become a daily addiction for me. So it was inevitable that those risks would increase exponentially, and eventually I would get caught. That day arrived when I was about forty-four and I received a tearful phone call at work from my wife informing me that she had discovered gay porn on our browser and could I explain why. Of course, once I'd got home, I had had time to invent an excuse. Yet again, the strength of courage had escaped me, and I didn't seize hold of the opportunity to admit who and what I was.

I had temporarily convinced my wife of my fidelity, as it were, and we therefore continued with the marriage as if nothing had happened, but the rot had set in, and my wife was certainly now suspicious. I changed my Internet trawling routine and methodically cleared out my browsing history, but I became complacent and lazy, and about six months later I forgot one day, and yes, that was the day she happened to discover the gay porn yet again. This time the matter wasn't discussed further, as my wife had now firmly made up her mind that I was gay. Though I didn't actually discover this until some eighteen months after we'd separated.

Just after I turned forty-six, we eventually did separate, but not until after a great deal of tears and upset and stress. I moved out of the family home and into a rented, two-bedroom flat. I was now living on my own for the first time in my life and had every opportunity to be a gay man, yet those old fears just wouldn't let it happen – I was no more happy as a gay man than I was as a straight or bisexual one.

After moving out, my mind was all over the place and I needed to get myself together for the sake of the children. My wife hadn't taken the separation well, or so I thought, and was sleeping around and dating any guy that looked at her twice. Surely that's what I should have been doing as well, but instead I was having to stay strong and form a daily routine for the children. They were struggling with life as it was, and to top all this I had just started a new job.

Eighteen months or so after we separated, some mum-friends asked me one Friday evening if I had started dating yet and if not, why not? As it happened, one of their divorcee friends had commented that she quite liked me, and after a few drinks, a couple of them got the idea of setting us up on a blind date. That very day I'd just been told by another friend that she'd heard a rumour that the reason why my wife and I had separated was on the account of me being gay. My heart stopped. I panicked and laughed it off, particularly when she said my wife had started saying this immediately after we'd been separated. Once again, an opportunity for me to be honest with myself and others – for me to come out – was presented, and I avoided it. So when my mum-friends suggested the blind date, I immediately said yes, on the grounds that it would ensure I could maintain my heterosexual image. The relationship lasted three months, but fell apart, as my heart wasn't truly in it, and one's performance in the bedroom doesn't come up to muster if you are no longer turned on by a woman. Needless to say, the lady in question realised something wasn't connecting between us and suggested we end things. We have bumped into each other a few times in the last twelve months, and if she ever suspected anything, she's never let on.

A couple of months after we ended things, I found myself feeling pretty low one Sunday afternoon, and no matter what I tried to do, I just couldn't get myself out of the doldrums. I went for a drive and the tears just wouldn't stop coming. I was surrounded by friends and had four children, but I hadn't ever felt so alone before in my entire life. You think stupid thoughts at times like this, but thankfully I quickly dismissed them, and anyway I'm such a coward. I was sure there must be other guys like me, but where were they? So when I got back home, I immediately went on the Internet and Googled for any UK-based gay dad support groups. That's when I found Gads UK, a membership-based website for gay dads, and my mood immediately lifted.

Through the website I met a Gad (as we call ourselves) based in London, and he introduced me to all the things I'd been missing all those years.

So I'm now in the midst of coming out, and it was my intention to come out to my kids over one weekend. Well, typically events have a tendency to overtake you. On the Thursday evening I officially came out to my ex-wife, though clearly she knew, hence the divorce, and I wanted to discuss with her how I planned on telling the kids and what, if any, concerns she had. The meeting went well and she agreed it was time for me to start living my life as me.

My eldest told me that my ex-wife and her boyfriend went to the pub and got slaughtered then came home and told whichever child of my middle two who was still awake, that their father was gay, and by all accounts they left nothing out. A huge argument between my eldest and her mum ensued, as my daughter was outraged that my ex-wife had taken my right to tell the children away from me. (Love her so much for that). My twelve-year-old daughter was upset, as she tends to see everything in black and white and couldn't quite get her head around it all, though she did have her suspicions. Her only comment was that she didn't want the kids at school to know. My fifteen-year-old son, who at the moment is like most fifteen-year-olds and only grunts and thinks the whole of society is against him, just shrugged and said, 'And?' My nine-year-old son slept through the whole thing, thus leaving just him for me to come out to.

I spoke with my twelve-year-old, who said that she doesn't care if I like women or if I like men, she still loves me, but can I be like the two gay hairdressers on Gogglebox because they're really funny.

I explained in as simple terms as I could to my nine-year-old, reminding him that I love him and will always be his dad, no matter what. He hugged me and I asked if he understood what I meant, and he said, 'Yes Dad, you're gay.'

Finally, when my fifteen-year-old came home from his mate's, I asked him how he felt about what his mum had told him. Bless him, he gave me a huge hug and a kiss and said, 'I love you, Dad, no matter what.'

Some three months after I first came out, I plucked up the courage, whilst on a visit north, to come out to my seventy-odd-year-old dad and my younger (twenty-two years in the army) brother, convinced that I'd be a total disappointment to them and likely banished forever to live in the south and never darken either of their doorways again. Typically, neither reacted as I'd anticipated, and whilst I doubt it's what my dad really wanted to hear, their love for me came through any other feelings or thoughts they might have had. In fact, as far as my two nephews were concerned, it just wasn't an issue.

So what the hell was I afraid of all this time? My kids and family are fine with it. I'm sure there will be wobbles along the way, but it's such a relief to let them all know and to be 'honest' at last. I'd built a huge protective wall around myself, but it was so high and so thick I was blind to the people around me and the changes in society over the past ten to fifteen years. I was always afraid to put my head over the top of that wall in case of being shot down. So far, I've had nothing but support and love from those I have told. The world is full of bigots and it always will be, but if our paths cross, I have no fear of them and I will handle each situation as fits best.

Life is good, no, life is great and has never been better, especially with someone special by my side supporting, encouraging and loving me all the way. He recently popped the question. I said yes, and my kids are so excited about it it's difficult to reconcile who I am now with who I was for all those years, until a relatively short time ago.

As for my fellow Gads, guys, thank you to each and every one of you, it's great to know there are caring similar people out there who understand and have your back.

*Note: Clause 28 – (quote from Wikipedia)

Section 28, or Clause 28 of the Local Government Act 1988, caused the addition of Section 2A to the Local Government Act 1986 which affected England, Wales and Scotland. The amendment was enacted on 24 May 1988, and stated that a local authority 'shall not intentionally promote homosexuality or publish material with the intention of promoting homosexuality', or 'promote the teaching in any maintained school of the acceptability of homosexuality as a pretended family relationship'. It was repealed on 21 June 2000 in Scotland as one of the first pieces of legislation enacted by the new Scottish Parliament, and on 18 November 2003 in the rest of the United Kingdom by section 122 of the Local Government Act 2003. As it did not create a criminal offence, no prosecution was ever brought under this provision, but its existence caused many groups to close or limit their activities or self-censor. For example, a number of lesbian, gay and bisexual student support groups in schools and colleges across Britain were closed owing to fears by council legal staff that they could breach the act.

Sex & Pornography

Pornography is a means to an end, if only relieving, but what it does so effectively is trigger physical responses to acts we are viewing that we would otherwise find at the least very uncomfortable and, at worst, abhorrent in our own bedrooms. But pornography is not a new phenomenon. We see it in the Roman bathhouses and the Indian *Kama Sutra*, and the latest technology has always been popularised by its capabilities to deliver pornographic images to us with such apparent ease – the Georgian postcard, Victorian photography and Edwardian cinematography all peddled lurid carnal images right at the very start.

Books too have always been a medium for telling explicitly sexual tales, often disguised in ambiguity, but those such as *Fifty Shades of Grey*, which would have been banned from the bookshelves like *Lady Chatterley's Lover* not that long ago, now fulfil the innermost hidden fantasies of millions of women, who under any other circumstance would find the ideas of S & M bondage as portrayed in the book as laughable, creepy or downright scary and dangerous in real life. It pushes all the right buttons, and that is what porn, soft or hard, does so intimately well, reducing us by our lack of physical participation to silent sexual pariahs.

It seems we humans have an innate fascination for watching or reading about other people putting their bodies and body parts to ever more contorted and extravagant sexual use, and they do it just for us, or that is the impression we get from the safety of our chair or bed as we watch and digest. Sex is a powerful emotion and from that first click on the mouse or the first turn of the page into a slowly building scene of raunchy sex, we begin the same cycle of phases we go through when we are having actual 'real' sex – excitement, plateau, orgasm and resolution.

Characteristics of the excitement phase, which we can make last for anything from a few minutes to several hours if we choose to, include:

- Muscle tension
- Heart rate quickening and breathing accelerating
- Skin may become flushed (blotches of redness appear on the chest and back)
- Nipples become hard or erect
- Blood flow to the penis causes erection

- Testicles swell, the scrotum tightens, and the penis begins secreting a lubricant or 'pre-cum' liquid

The plateau phase, which extends to the brink of orgasm, includes:

- Phase one changes intensified
- The testicles withdraw up into the scrotum
- Breathing, heart rate, and blood pressure all continue to increase
- Muscle spasms might begin, especially in the legs
- Muscle tension increases

Orgasm is the climax of the sexual-response cycle. It is the shortest of the phases and generally lasts only a few seconds and includes:

- Involuntary muscle contractions
- Blood pressure, heart rate, and breathing are all at their highest rates, with a rapid intake of oxygen
- Muscles in the feet spasm
- There is a sudden, forceful release of sexual tension

- Rhythmic contractions of the muscles at the base of the penis result in the ejaculation of semen
- A flush may appear over the entire body

During resolution phase, the body slowly returns to normal. The erect penis returns to its previous size and colour, and this phase is marked by a general sense of well-being and fatigue.

Pornography works because it has little to do with intellect, it works simply on our biological responses like most drugs or stimulants that cause a rush of endorphins. Whether you are a Lord of the Realm or an unemployed teenager out of school with zero qualifications, the high is just the same. What most of us are able to do, however, is lead a normal, unaffected life despite having porn as our occasional virtual partner. Once orgasm has been reached, most men can get on with things without thinking any more about it, but, and this is the big problem with a modern technologically based society such as ours, overexposure to graphic sex deadens the senses, and the addiction of it requires us to view more and more and increasingly graphic to get that same fix.

Porn

(by TV presenter Alistair Appleton www.alistairappleton.com/blog)

I went on a whim last night to see the excellent Chris Green (from Duckie) and his new show *Prurience*, which was part of the Sick! Festival in Brighton. It wasn't purely by chance since the blurb in the festival brochure talked about an immersive evening exploring the nature of porn addiction, which is a subject I'm interested in both personally and professionally.

As a gay man growing up in a pre-Internet age, my exposure to porn was probably typical in being a few feverishly hoarded pictures and then, later, when I was more ballsy, a carefully curated collection of gay magazines, stories and cartoon books. In a period of UK history when being gay was demonised, these images and stories probably carved a space for some semblance of erotic life to grow. I didn't see a pornographic film until some fumbled moments in a cabin on the Rue St. Denis in Paris when I was twenty-two – it took a lot of one-franc coins, as I remember.

The advent of Internet chatrooms in the '90s (dialling up CompuServe after peak hours, anyone?) led to the beginnings of a more 'interactive' titillation. But this was pure innocence compared to the supernova of porn that has erupted all over the Web in the last five years. High-speed Internet access is the fuel. I got burned by that for a while and managed to escape the worst ravages of this epidemic, but I have clients who have fared less well. This is not the playful erotica of yesteryear, but porn on an industrial scale aimed perfectly at the slavish synapses of modern consumers.

The combination of sex, almost infinite novelty and privacy makes modern porn consumption a lethal cocktail for brain chemistry. The brain's SEEKING system (as described by Panksepp) is wired entirely to enjoy and explore novelty and chase. It is the system that is fired up by cocaine and it is regulated by dopamine. It's pleasurable and it supersedes other bigger-picture views while it's fired up. Most significantly, it is a quite different system from the SATISFACTION system, which is largely ruled by opioids.

Consumer capitalism thrives on a constant stimulation of the SEEKING system and a minimisation of the SATISFACTION system. Business and commerce are not interested in our being satisfied, they want us to be constantly seeking, and so any product that ruthlessly stimulates the dopamine system is like a gold mine. Pornography is the silver bullet. It stimulates the sex-seeking system; sites like PornTube allow access to almost infinite short clips, so the novelty button is also pushed; issues of shame and embarrassment mean that the satisfaction of orgasm is rarely pleasurable and preferably delayed, which leads to marathon sessions of 'edging'.

Industrial Internet porn leaves people (often men) uniquely vulnerable to the predatory incursions of consumer capitalism. With the long-term prospects of unemployment, educational debt and impoverishment on the horizon for lots of young males in the affluent West, getting lost in a sticky haze of porn might seem like a good hole to hide in.

You may well bridle at the idea that we should feel sorry for these people who are locked into hours and hours of increasingly hard-core and brain-corroding porn consumption, but I think this is a really large and as-yet undiscussed issue.

I was amazed that there seems to be a dismissal at the connection between this industrial-scale consumption of porn and erectile dysfunction, but there are masses of circumstantial evidence and native testimony that describes a very precise link between the constant viewing of hard-core porn and a massive decrease in the ability of users to respond to real people – girlfriends or boyfriends –

in sexual situations. They can reach orgasm with porn, but suffer erectile dysfunction with real lovers.

I am aware that as a Buddhist meditator, I have a particular axe to grind here. It's not a moral thing but rather an existential one. You could style the project of meditation as a recalibration of life from concept to reality, so naturally I am very much on the side of real, messy, challenging, skin-on-skin sex, rather than the safe and self-circuited nature of porn, but I am conscious that other people might have a different view on it. My tendency is – admittedly – to radical realism, but I can imagine that some people have a more nuanced understanding of the power of image and word.

In either case, Chris Green's piece is a great experience – teetering on the edge of too much meta-theatricality, but outlining a really interesting area that I agree needs much more discussion if we're not going to end up with a psycho-sexual time bomb ticking under our noses.

Porn Addiction

Porn addiction is a subsection of sex addiction and refers to the excessive use of porn to the point that it has a negative impact on the life of the user and often those around him. The use of legal porn sites is massive: 20 per cent of men admit to viewing porn even whilst at work. The vast majority of those users, however, are not addicted.

In the UK in 2013, porn websites were being accessed more than all social networks and shopping networks combined; and according to the Public Policy Research survey:

- 70 per cent of UK teenagers say that porn is seen as normal by their peers at school
- 46 per cent of teenagers said sexting is a part of everyday life for people their age
- Two out of three girls and nearly 50 per cent of boys said growing up would be easier if porn was harder to access

According to an Opinium Survey of eighteen-year-olds, they also felt under intense pressure to conform to pornographic norms. An astonishing 80 per cent said it was too easy to stumble across explicit images and videos on the Internet.

Traffic to legal porn sites in the UK comprised 8.5 per cent of all clicks-throughs on web pages. Only 'arts and entertainment', a category that is boosted by YouTube, at 9.5 per cent of the category and others which make up 15.7 per cent of the category, were bigger. The figures, which do not include traffic from mobile phones – of which one in five Internet searches via a phone are for porn – were compiled by SimilarWeb, by tracking clicks online rather than total volume of traffic.

Internationally, it appears that Britain is less interested in porn than Germany, where it makes up 12.5 per cent of traffic, nearly half as much again as in the UK, and somewhat less than Spain, where it comprises 9.6 per cent. Britain ranks above the world average, however, of 7.7 per cent, and slightly ahead of the US, where adult traffic makes up 8.3 per cent of clicks.

Internet service providers have been given the challenge by the Prime Minister, of ensuring that anyone signing up for an Internet service would have to choose whether to opt in or out of being able to access pornographic sites, but this still doesn't tackle the issue of addiction.

Can watching porn or reading books or magazines with sexual content ever be considered 'healthy' or at the least non-harmful? This is a topic for debate in which there is no clear answer. Some will say that watching porn to any degree is harmful and demoralising because the watcher is fuelling the need for porn to be made in the first place, thereby creating an industry in which those who are filmed are themselves degraded and sometimes violently abused.

The signs or symptoms of porn addiction might include:

- Excessive viewing of porn – 'excessive' depends on what is healthy or not, but generally it is when the impact on normal everyday life has become detrimental
- Watching porn interferes with daily life, responsibilities and routines
- More time is spent watching porn or searching for more stimulating porn to get you aroused or to orgasm. You develop a tolerance and require stronger, harder porn to satisfy your need to climax
- Afterwards there is a feeling of emotional distress or withdrawal because the session has ended
- You continue to use porn despite other serious consequences, such as break down

of relationships, disciplining at work or even losing your job

- Compulsive masturbation – again 'compulsive' depends on what one would consider healthy or not. Some religions would argue that any masturbation is unhealthy, but generally, compulsive is taken to mean, as the definition in the Oxford English Dictionary states: 'resulting from or acting on an irresistible urge or compulsion'. Compulsion means: 'to behave in a certain way, especially against one's conscious wishes'.
- Sexual dysfunction, i.e., impotence, premature ejaculation
- Negative effects on relationships, i.e., difficult to become aroused by your partner, sexual behaviour becomes more aggressive or dominant or emotionally disconnected
- Porn becomes a release to alter your mood, especially if changing feelings of depression or anxiety

What causes porn addiction?

Porn addiction, like any other substance dependence, can be understood through the principles of conditioning, where behaviour is reinforced by reward. Porn is highly reinforcing because it taps into a very basic instinct – sexual reward.

When having sex or watching porn, dopamine is released into a part of the brain that handles emotion and learning, and gives a sense of focus and craving 'to know more'. We get a great sense of pleasure from this, and the next time we feel horny, dopamine is released and the brain tells us 'remember last time you felt like this, go there and get it'. Anything that gives us pleasure is positively shunted forward by the release of dopamine, whether that be eating or exercising or sex. The more addictive or pleasurable to us something is, the more dopamine is released. So the more porn you watch, the more dopamine is dispersed into the brain, and the more you crave or need it, until there comes a point, as with any addiction, that you simply 'require' the fix of dopamine, the feeling of the high. Visualising those images you see on the computer when you are away from it reinforces them, and the orgasm you get whilst watching them intensifies, releasing even more dopamine, which then strengthens the connections in your brain made during the session. The cycle can then be hard to escape, and just like a drug, your tolerance towards the visual stimulation becomes anesthetised, and the need for more and more stronger doses leads to it becoming more difficult to be turned on by a real partner.

Another hormone, norepinephrine, is also released into the brain, which creates alertness. It's similar to adrenaline and it tells the brain to 'get ready, something really great is about to happen and you need to be ready for it'. Oxytocin and vasopressin are also released, binding the memory of the object that gives us the sexual pleasure to the cells. The body then releases endorphins, which are natural highs like opiates and which bring a wave of pleasure and well-being. After orgasm, serotonin levels change, bringing a sense of calm and fulfilment.

All these hormones work perfectly in conjunction, as they are meant to, whilst having sex with a partner, but porn short-circuits the system. The high and alertness of sexual pleasure and the deep calm afterwards cannot be reciprocated by a computer screen, but in effect that is what is happening because porn rewards us so effectively.

How to stop porn addiction?

Persistent behaviours such as porn addiction often suggest an absence of something else. While it is important not to completely ignore the addictive behaviour, often the journey towards a better balance in life is through focussing on other aspects, sometimes relationships, sometimes other feelings that are desperate to be explored and heard. Often addictive behaviours are a way for men to cover up or hide away from something else in their lives they don't feel they can deal with. For some men, they may not be aware of what these other issues are, or even that they exist.

Porn addictions can occur in cycles. There can be times when accessing it happens very often, and then there may be other times when the need for it is not so strong, or life is interesting and busy, or it might simply be because there is not the opportunity. Setting goals, such as 'I'm not going to do it for seven days', or even giving yourself a reward at the end: 'if I abstain for two weeks, I'll reward myself with ….' can significantly reduce the desire. The brain works on the 'use it or lose it' principle, where connections and memories are made and reinforced through constant use. Stop using porn and the connections that have been made gradually fade and the desire to stimulate these feelings again become weaker and less all-consuming.

Because of the nature of porn addiction, it can be really hard for many men to seek help from those close to them. If you feel that porn is an issue in your life, try to seek some support and help from a qualified professional, but in the first instance you should talk to your doctor.

This is Chris' Story

I often get asked how I ended up marrying a woman and having children even though I knew I was gay. I guess there's not a straightforward answer to this, but one that has several factors that delayed my coming out until my early thirties.

With hindsight, I always knew I was different from the other boys at school, and I was always attracted to boys and men from my earliest recollections. This became more apparent as puberty and hormones kicked in and I started to notice other boys, especially in the showers after PE lessons.

I had a 'Christian' upbringing, which was strongly influenced by my mother. I can't say that I ever felt judged as a child by my parents with regards to being different; however, growing up during the 1970s and '80s, it was still not socially acceptable to be openly gay or lesbian, and it was certainly not legal to get married or start a family if the two of you were homosexuals.

I was a very sensitive and emotional boy, and over the years I received casual comments from my peers about me being a 'homo' or a 'poof', and I guess there were occasions when I overheard my parents' friends or family members comment about people in the town they suspected of being gay or lesbian, and then would laugh. At church the attitude was similarly judgemental, and what prevailed was that anything other than a heterosexual marriage was basically sinful and not a valid choice.

On television during the 1970s and '80s, there were male entertainers and actors such as John Inman, Liberace, Danny La Rue and Larry Grayson who were 'effeminate' and clearly gay. However, with the overwhelming culture at the time still being socially unacceptable to be openly gay, I never saw these men as role models. The language often used amongst heterosexual men and women was that they weren't 'real men', whatever that means. They were always seen as a joke because they were camp and not traditionally masculine.

As I grew up, my homosexual feelings and thoughts developed, but I never considered that I could admit to anyone that I was gay. As a teenager, I thought I would be seen as a joke and not a so-called 'real man'. I never thought it would be possible to kiss or have sex with another man. I was ashamed of my thoughts. I never considered that same-sex couples were valid relationships or that I could have a same-sex relationship or that it could be viewed as acceptable.

In my early twenties, family and friends started to enquire about my dating, with the usual questions: 'So, any lucky ladies in your life?' and 'When are you going to settle down? ... get married? ... have kids?' I just went along with it and made jokes back about not finding the right woman. To be honest, due to my shyness and uncertainty of my sexuality, I didn't even kiss anyone until I was twenty-one. I had a romantic idea of getting married to a woman and always had the desire to be a dad. The thought of having children one day was definitely something I wanted.

In my final year at university I decided to confide in a few friends that I fancied guys. The responses were mixed. Some Christian friends were instantly condemning and judgemental: 'You can't be gay, it's sinful', 'You'll go to Hell!' they said. Others were much more compassionate and didn't really see it as an issue. I was all prepared for 'coming out' despite not having met anyone special (male or female) that had changed my conviction that I was gay.

Just when I had started to make sense of my sexuality, I was introduced to my now ex-wife, via a friend. Initially we struck up a great friendship and spent lots of time together. She knew that I might be gay, but did not seem bothered by this. At the time I didn't really want a physical relationship with her, I was just so elated to find someone who understood me and shared lots of similar values and ambitions in life. It was during this period of dating a woman that I ended up having my first gay sexual experience.

It was in the lead-up to my graduation ball in my final year at university that I had started noticing a guy around campus who I fancied, and he seemed to be interested in me. Coincidentally, he was one of the organisers of the ball, and whenever I finished lectures, he always seemed to be walking down the corridor, being openly flirty with me, but due to my shyness and guilt about my sexuality, I never reciprocated.

As all my other friends were taking a partner, I decided to take my girlfriend to the ball as my date. We started drinking as soon as we arrived, and within a short time I had got very drunk. Once the meal had finished, I went to the toilet. When I got there, I noticed that the guy who had been flirting with me in the past few weeks was standing at one of the urinals. I guess it was because my guard was down due to the inebriation that I started talking to him, and the conversation very quickly turned into passionate kissing in one of the toilet cubicles.

This was such an amazing, electric experience. For the first time, I had fulfilled a fantasy of kissing a man, and

I felt so alive – the most alive I had felt up until that point. We decided that the cubicle was probably too obvious a place to be getting intimate, especially as I was not out and my date was in the next room. We found a darkened corridor and ended up making out for at least half an hour. I didn't want it to end, but I had abandoned my girlfriend with strangers whilst I was getting off with a guy, and I was racked with guilt and shame. I was exhilarated, but totally taken aback by this unplanned encounter, and I had been a bad boyfriend by being unfaithful.

This was a very conflicting time for me. I had finally fulfilled a fantasy, to kiss a man and be intimate with him, whilst at the same time I had started dating a girl and was feeling guilty for cheating on her and for acting on my gay feelings.

I had been away from the dinner table for a long time, and my date had become concerned of my whereabouts and had been asking after me. Someone had said they'd seen me talking to a guy in the toilets, and she worked out that I had probably been doing a lot more than just talking.

Naturally she was angry and upset with me and wanted to know what had happened and how I felt about us as a couple. We decided to sleep on it and talk the next day.

I had a sleepless night due to feeling enormously guilty and also being dreadfully hungover. After battling my thoughts and emotions all night, I asked her to come over to my house to talk. I had decided that the best thing for me to do was to apologise to her, but also to end our relationship. I couldn't cope with the idea of cheating on her and letting her down. I was also conflicted about whether I could maintain a relationship with a woman when I had now been intimate with a man. It was one of the worst moments in my life to have to tell her what I had decided, because I still loved her and cared for her, but I just thought she was better off without me. Consequently, we split up and agreed not to keep in contact.

I graduated from university that month and moved back with my parents to find a job. It took me months to get over that night. I had regular dreams recalling this first sexual encounter with another man and feeling exhilarated; however, upon waking, I was then racked with guilt and couldn't stop thinking about how I had hurt a lovely woman who had done nothing to deserve being treated that way.

I continued to attend the church near my parents' and still believed in God, and I would pray regularly. Part of my prayers was asking God to stop or change my gay feelings so that I could be a 'normal' straight guy and get married. I guess I had always naively hoped, deep down in my heart, that somehow God would 'heal' me of these gay feelings.

At that time my logic was this: that if God sees being gay as sinful and wrong, then surely He would want to change me to make me acceptable? During this period, some well-meaning but misguided people in the church counselled and advised me that God would 'heal' me of my homosexual feelings. I even had one pastor tell me that I was possessed and that this 'rebellious spirit' within me was what caused me to be attracted to men. I was horrified by that thought – how could a decent Christian guy like me be essentially evil and possessed by a spirit?

It was at this point I started to hate myself for being gay, and I resigned myself to a life of compromise, trying to suppress my gay feelings and starting to 'act straight'.

I was missing talking to my ex-girlfriend and really wanted to try to make amends with her. I thought that if we were at least friends again, I would feel better about myself and what I had done.

I wrote to her to ask for forgiveness, explaining that I really missed her and how terrible I felt for being unfaithful to her. After a couple of weeks, I got a reply in the post. She was still very hurt and angry towards me, but she seemed to be willing to at least be on friendly terms again. Over the next few months we started writing regularly and speaking on the phone. She made me feel so good about myself, and even though I didn't really feel a sexual attraction to her, I decided that we had a great friendship that I didn't want to lose.

She obviously felt the same about our friendship, and we soon began to visit each other. Our parents and friends started to ask about our relationship, and after a month or so of dating again, her father, who was a church minister, asked me what my intentions were for his daughter. With hindsight I understand that her father was simply looking out for his daughter; however, I felt very intimidated by this question, as I didn't really have a plan in my head beyond seeing how things developed between us. After a few more prompts from her and her parents, I realised that I had to decide what I wanted. Did I want to be single again and hate myself for being a 'sinful gay', or did I pluck up the courage to get engaged and conform to what everyone else wanted?

I decided that being single and dealing with my 'sinful' feelings was too painful to think about. Here was a woman who wanted to share her life with me and was excited about having children with me in the future. So I plucked up the courage and proposed to her, and the next day we announced to family and friends that we were getting married.

In 1998, after both of us completed our university studies, we got married and moved in together to start our life as a married couple. We had a 'three-year plan', which involved both of us taking time to focus on each other and our new careers as professionals. This would allow us to save up some money for a deposit to purchase our first house.

Nine months into our marriage, my wife announced, rather stunned and tearfully, that our plan would need to be amended. She was pregnant and expecting our first daughter. Naturally, after the initial shock of the news, we were both over the moon at the idea of becoming parents, and our daughter arrived nine months later, two weeks before the Millennium. Despite the initial shock of sleepless nights and all the dirty nappies, I loved being a dad and I felt like my life was complete with my wife and new baby daughter. With working full time and being a parent, I didn't have time to think, so my anxieties about being gay were pushed to the back of my mind.

When my wife discovered she was pregnant with our second daughter, she began to experience numerous health problems during the pregnancy. She was working full time as a teacher, mum to our daughter, and pregnant. She was not really in the mood to be affectionate and understandably didn't want to entertain the idea of sex. I realised that as her husband, I needed to be supportive, but I think that due to my low self-esteem and also a desire to receive affection, my homosexual feelings started to surface again. Initially, I pushed them aside, but they seemed much stronger than before. I felt incredibly guilty for thinking about men whilst I was married and also because I was a Christian.

After a few months of this internal battle, I gradually sank into a depression. I had serious doubts about my faith and was having strong homosexual desires. I eventually spoke to my wife about my struggles. Even though she knew about them before we got married, she was upset and naturally concerned about what I was going to do next. I decided to share my struggles with someone at church, and they told me about a Christian support group for men and women who struggled with homosexuality. I attended this group for about a year. I found it very cathartic to meet with these men and share our similar struggles. The group leaders were very compassionate men and had battled themselves with their Christian faith and homosexuality.

However, the main ethos of the group was that 'God hates the sin, not the sinner', or in other words, being gay or lesbian is fine, but acting out your homosexual desires and having a gay relationship is wrong and sinful. I struggled with this. Why should God or anyone else tell me that I could have homosexual feelings but never act on them? As a married man, I didn't want to be unfaithful to my wife, but I couldn't ignore these very strong desires I had to be intimate with another man anymore. I felt I had to make a decision. I really wanted to make my wife and God happy, but I was also so miserable and depressed.

Our second daughter was born in 2004. My wife made a full recovery from the pregnancy, and life with the four of us became even fuller. Both of us worked full time, as well as having two little ones under five, and it started to take its toll on us, as neither of us had much energy or time at the end of each day.

Rather than being open about my sexual struggles, I gradually started to withdraw. I began to research about being gay on the Internet and discovered gay dating sites as well as porn. I felt disgusting for doing this behind my wife's back and just imagined how judgemental my Christian friends would be, but the strong desire to be with a man became all-consuming. I started chatting to gay men online, but hid my identity for fear of being discovered. After chatting to a few guys, I decided that if I had never really acted on my gay feelings, how could I definitely know for sure that I was gay. My only experience with a man had been years earlier at university.

I eventually started chatting to a gay man online who wanted to meet me for sex. I arranged to meet him, and before long we ended up in bed together. I felt extremely guilty for having done this, but at the same time it was so exhilarating and fulfilling. I stayed in touch briefly, but I was too messed up to attempt a relationship, so I stopped messaging him. Despite this, I now knew I had to be honest with myself and my wife, and admit that I was gay. This was the toughest and scariest decision I had ever made in my life.

I began to think about the consequences and repercussions of coming out. I was terrified. I was heartbroken that I could lose my wife – my best friend. She was the only person in the world who I had shared my inner thoughts and my life with, and despite no sex life, we still had a strong friendship. If she took it really badly, I might also lose access to my daughters, and what would our friends at church and other family and friends say?

Despite all these fears, I was sick of living a lie and pretending to my wife and everyone else that I was someone else. I could only see me becoming more withdrawn and repressed and this turning into bitterness and resentment. I wanted to give my wife the chance to meet another man who could give her what she wanted and not live a lie, and I didn't want my children to see their dad become so negative. It was draining me of all positivity and life. I was using up all my energy trying to maintain a crumbling façade. It had to stop.

Telling my wife that I couldn't go on any more, my heart was pounding and I felt physically sick. She was obviously heartbroken. Once she had calmed down, she suggested that we try some marriage counselling. I felt that this was rather pointless, but I guess I thought it may be useful. We tried this for two weeks, but by this time I was resolute and told her of my intentions. She asked me to leave our family home. The image of my ex-wife and my tiny daughters all crying as I left still haunts me today. Seeing them sobbing made me feel like the most despicable villain in any movie. I felt numb. Was I really doing this? Where was I going to live? Would I see my daughters again? I was absolutely heartbroken and had so many emotions spinning around in my head. Feelings of huge relief mixed with feelings of tremendous guilt. I felt like I would cry forever and couldn't see a happy ending to this big mess. At the age of thirty-three, I was leaving behind my wife and two children to start a new life.

I decided I needed to share what had happened with someone else, so dropped in on some friends. (These friends have been absolute rocks to me, and without their support, I would not be here today.) I turned up, a dishevelled mess, on my friends' doorstep. Thankfully, they took me in, gave me hugs and listened to my story. They did not take sides or pass judgement on what I had done, and they offered me a place to stay whilst I sorted out things with my wife and children.

It was very raw to begin with, telling others that we were separating. I felt a total failure because my marriage was ending and I had hurt the closest people to me. Initially, I was reluctant to tell other people about my sexuality as well as the divorce, because I was scared of possible rejection. However, I gradually told my family and friends about the divorce, and as people started asking the reasons why, I thought I might as well 'come out' to them at the same time. It saved explaining things twice and I was getting sick of repeating the same story. I am relieved to say that the majority of them were very supportive and understanding.

The separation and divorce proceedings were slow, and the relationship between my wife and me became very strained. Thankfully she was fine about me having equal access to my daughters, and we agreed that I would have them on alternate weekends to stay over. I was so happy with this arrangement because it meant I would still be able to have an active role in my children's life. This period was a roller coaster of emotions. I was elated to be free, to date other guys and start being more open with others, yet at the same time, I felt so guilty and upset at instigating the break-up. Each time I said goodbye to my daughters, I sobbed, knowing that we would not all be living together as a family unit again. After eighteen months of emotional turmoil and legal process, the divorce finally came through. On the day I received the decree nisi, I actually felt quite mixed emotions about it. I was relieved that we could both now legally move on with our lives, but at the same time I still remained sad and guilty over the divorce.

Since then, relations have improved between my ex-wife and me. My children have slowly adapted to seeing me separately from their mum.

Nine years have now passed since the separation, and so much has happened for us as a family. I have had disagreements with my ex-wife, but we have managed to stay amicable. We have always supported each other with the disciplining of our children, and despite numerous attempts by our girls to play us off against each other, we have managed to stay united. I still have regular access to my children and have them on alternate weekends and school holidays.

I have been honest with my girls about my sexuality. I decided not to make a big statement but rather allow them to ask questions in their own time. My eldest daughter is now almost sixteen and loves to discuss her boy-band crushes with me. She often asks me whether I fancy a male celebrity on TV or a man in the street. I find it all quite entertaining and I am so glad that I can freely discuss these things without fear of judgement or hatred.

People have asked me if I regret getting married and not coming out as gay earlier; of course, my answer is not at all. I had a great few years being married to my wife and I enjoyed setting up a home together for our family. We made each other laugh and supported each other through a few tough times. On our wedding day, I genuinely believed that we were getting married for life and that things would always work out for the best. I am so grateful every day for the fact that I have two beautiful daughters. Being a parent is challenging for anyone and some days it can be very hard, but my children make my life so much richer.

I am currently single, but I am 500% happier than I was pretending to be someone else. I am happy being me: openly gay and no longer living in hiding. My kids, family and friends know that I am gay and are all very supportive.

Homosexuality & Religion

Judaism

The Torah is the primary source for Jewish views on homosexuality. It states that: '[A man] shall not lie with another man as [he would] with a woman, it is an 'abomination'' (Leviticus 18:22). Like many similar commandments, the punishment for wilful violation is the death penalty. In practice, though, rabbinic Judaism no longer believes it has the authority to implement death penalties. In recent years it has been claimed that only the sexual anal act is forbidden and considered an abomination by the Torah, but as anal intercourse is practised more widely amongst heterosexuals, this 'sin' should not be laid at the feet of homosexuals exclusively. People's sexual orientation and even other sexual activities are not considered a sin. The official position is to welcome homosexual Jews into the synagogues, and to campaign against any discrimination in civil law and public society.

Reform Judaism and Liberal Judaism in the United Kingdom view homosexuality to be acceptable on the same basis as heterosexuality. Progressive Jewish authorities believe either that traditional laws against homosexuality are no longer binding or that they are subject to changes that reflect a new understanding of human sexuality. Some of these authorities rely on modern biblical scholarship, which suggests that the prohibition in the Torah was intended to ban coercive or ritualized homosexual sex, such as those practices ascribed to Egyptian and Canaanite fertility cults and temple prostitution.

Christianity

Christian denominations hold a variety of views on the issue of homosexual activity, ranging from outright condemnation to complete acceptance. Most Christian denominations welcome people attracted to the same sex, but teach that homosexual acts are sinful.

The Anglican Communion, which includes the Church of England, have struggled with the controversy of homosexuality since the late 1980s and has formerly expressed its position on two occasions. Firstly, in November 1987, the General Synod passed by 403 votes to 8 the following motion:

'That this Synod affirms that the biblical and traditional teaching on chastity and fidelity in personal relationships in a response to, and expression of, God's love for each one of us, and in particular affirms:

1. that sexual intercourse is an act of total commitment which belongs properly within a permanent married relationship

2. that fornication and adultery are sins against this ideal, and are to be met by a call to repentance and the exercise of compassion

3. that homosexual genital acts also fall short of this ideal, and are likewise to be met by a call to repentance and the exercise of compassion

4. that all Christians are called to be exemplary in all spheres of morality, including sexual morality; and that holiness of life is particularly required of Christian leaders'

In December 1991, the House of Bishops (the Synod) published *Issues in Human Sexuality*. This endorsed the traditional Christian belief that in the teaching of the Bible heterosexual marriage is the proper context for sexual activity between two people. It went on to declare:

'The convergence of Scripture, Tradition and reasoned reflection on experience, even including the newly sympathetic and perceptive thinking of our own day, makes it impossible for the Church to come with integrity to any other conclusion. Heterosexuality and homosexuality are not equally congruous with the observed order of creation or with the insights of revelation as the Church engages with these in the light of her pastoral ministry.'

It also argued that the decisions of those who enter into such relationships must be respected, and that the Church must 'not reject those who sincerely believe it is God's call to them'.

Because of the 'distinctive nature of their calling, status and consecration', the clergy 'cannot claim the liberty to enter into sexually active homophile relationships'.

The Roman Catholic Church

Homosexuality in the Roman Catholic Church is treated in two ways. Firstly, homosexual orientation is considered an 'objective disorder' because Catholicism views it as being 'ordered toward an intrinsic moral evil', but not sinful unless acted upon. Secondly, homosexual sexual activity, by contrast, is viewed as a 'moral disorder' and 'homosexual acts' as 'contrary to natural law' because, simply put, homosexuality closes the sexual act to the gift of life. Therefore, the Catholic church do not regard homosexual activity as a perfect expression of the sacrament of marriage, which it teaches is only possible within the lifelong commitment of a marriage between a man and a woman. It opposes the introduction of both civil and religious same-sex marriage. The Church also holds the belief that same-sex unions are an unfavourable environment for children to be brought up in and that the legalization of such unions is therefore harmful to society.

Islam

Islam is influenced by the religious, legal and cultural history of the nations which are comprised of sizable Muslim populations, along with specific passages in the Quran and statements, or Hadiths, attributed to the Islamic prophet Muhammad. Therefore, orthodox Islam is not only a system of beliefs, but also a legal system. Traditional schools of Islamic law based on Qur'anic verses consider homosexual acts a punishable crime and a sin. The Qur'an cites the story of the people of Lot and the cities of Sodom and Gomorrah destroyed by the wrath of God because they engaged in lustful acts between men. Nevertheless, homoerotic themes were present in poetry and other literature written by some Muslims from the mediaeval period onwards.

Today, in most of the Islamic world, homosexuality is not socially or legally accepted. In some of these countries – Afghanistan, Brunei, Iran, Mauritania, Nigeria,

Saudi Arabia, Sudan and Yemen – homosexual activity carries the death penalty. In others, such as Somalia and Malaysia, it is illegal. (See Anti-gay countries of the world.)

Hinduism

Hindu religion has taken various positions on homosexuality, ranging from positive to neutral or antagonistic. Referring to the nature of Samsara, the Rigveda, one of the four sacred texts of Hinduism, says 'perversity/diversity is what nature is all about, or, what seems unnatural is also natural'. Sexuality is rarely openly discussed in modern Hindu society, especially among the strongly religious. It is generally regarded that Hinduism as a whole does not condemn homosexuality.

A third gender, or the hijras, have long been acknowledged within Hinduism since Vedic times. Several Hindu texts, such as *Manu Smriti*, state that some people are born with either mixed male and female natures, or sexually neutral, as a matter of natural biology. These hijras traditionally worked as hairdressers, flower sellers, servants, masseurs and prostitutes. Today, many people of the third gender live throughout India, but mostly on the margins of society.

The *Kama Sutra*, written in 150 BC, contains passages describing eunuchs or 'third-sex' males performing oral sex on men. Similarly, some mediaeval Hindu temples and artefacts openly depict male homosexuality and lesbianism in their carvings, such as the temple walls at Khajuraho. Some infer from these images that at least part of Hindu society and religion were previously more open to variations in human sexuality than they are today.

Many Hindu divinities are androgynous, and others switch from male to female or from female to male. However, this is not accepted by the majority of Hindus and is often considered heretical in nature. Those who do accept it justify it with the belief that both God and nature are unlimitedly diverse and that God is difficult to comprehend.

Buddhism

In the early sutras of Buddhism, 'accepted or unaccepted human sexual conduct' for people is not specifically mentioned. Buddhism in its earliest form did not clearly define sexuality rules; instead it restricted the subject mostly to monks and their behaviour. Therefore, the determination of whether or not homosexuality is acceptable for the general populace is not considered to be a religious matter by many Buddhists. Still, there is a wide diversity of opinion about homosexuality. Buddhism teaches that sensual enjoyment and desire in general, and sexual pleasure in particular, are hindrances to enlightenment and inferior to the kinds of pleasure that are integral to the practice of meditation. However, most Buddhists do not pursue a life of meditation or aim for higher enlightenment. For most, the goal in their lives is to have a pleasant life, and after their deaths, a pleasant rebirth.

Regarding Buddhist monks, the Vinaya (the code of monastic discipline) bans all sexual activity, making no moral distinction among the many possible forms of intercourse it lists.

The current Dalai Lama, Tenzin Gyatso, follows the traditional Tibetan Buddhist assertion that inappropriate sexual behaviour includes lesbian and gay sex, and indeed any sex other than penis-vagina intercourse with one's own monogamous partner, this includes oral sex, anal sex, and masturbation. He has stated: 'If someone comes to me and asks whether homosexuality is okay or not, I will ask them, "What is your companion's opinion?" If they both agree, then I think I would say, "If two males or two females voluntarily agree to have mutual satisfaction without further implication of harming others, then it is okay."'

However, he later stated that 'homosexuality, whether it is between men or between women, is not improper in itself, what is improper is the use of organs already defined as inappropriate for sexual contact.' He also had difficulty in imagining the mechanics of homosexual sex, saying that nature had arranged male and female organs 'in such a manner that is very suitable ... Same-sex organs cannot manage well'.

Sikhism

Sikhism has no specific teachings about homosexuality. The Sikh holy book, the *Guru Granth Sahib*, does not explicitly mention homosexuality, and the universal goal of a Sikh is to have no hate or animosity to any person, regardless of factors like race, caste, colour, creed, gender, or sexuality. However, in 2005, a Sikh religious authority described homosexuality as 'against the Sikh religion and the Sikh code of conduct, and totally against the laws of nature', and called on Sikhs to support laws against gay marriage. Many Sikhs are against this view, however, and state that the Sikh Scriptures promote equality and do not condemn homosexuality. The partnership of marriage in Sikhism is seen as a union of souls and the soul is seen as genderless, the outward appearance of humans (men and women), merely a temporary state.

This is Deep's Story

I was born in London in the late 1970s into an Indian Sikh immigrant family. I had a large extended family, growing up amongst lots of cousins and within a close-knit community. This strong sense of family made me very comfortable, and there was an immensely powerful duty of responsibility to live up to the expectations of the family in particular, but also others. I felt completely overwhelmed by this; however, I would gently rebel in small ways. I knew education would be my way to break free from being under the complete influence of my domineering extended family, who were all heavily influenced by the matriarch of the family, my grandmother. My mum, on the other hand, was a completely refreshing and very powerful woman. She instilled within me great values, strength of conviction and belief in God.

External factors impacting on my adolescence were growing up in an ethnic minority and a very distinguishably identifiable religious minority too. As a turban-wearing Sikh I always stood out wherever I was. I remember at the age of ten going to visit family in India and being astonished that even there I stood out as a foreigner, even though I shared the same ethnicity as everyone else. So the resounding theme that I grew up with was that I was different.

Growing up in the 1980s, there was a lot of negativity around homosexuality. The only openly gay people were celebrities who dressed in drag and wore make-up and wildly outrageous clothes. None of them were identifiable by me as role models. This was then overshadowed by the ongoing bad press about HIV and AIDs being a 'gay disease' and church scandals involving child sexual abuse, etc. You couldn't be Indian and gay, let alone Sikh and gay. Although as a child I didn't think about my Sikh faith and sexuality together, the overall feeling was I couldn't be both gay and Sikh nor remain within the Sikh community as a gay man. They were definitely two distinctly different entities.

I wanted a family. I wanted a loving relationship. I wanted a 'normal' life. So subconsciously I ignored any feelings for men and buried them deep down inside me. If they were resurrected by any thoughts of admiring a man I saw, these feelings were buried even further.

So I continued growing up, dealing with issues of race, religion, ethnicity, but clearly ignoring sexuality. I managed to somehow ignore these feelings to such an extent that I had convinced myself that I was 'normal', that this was only a phase and it didn't bother me at all. I remember arriving at university, excited about the challenges that lay ahead and wanting to try new things, but I veered clear of the Gay Societies and groups.

Having graduated, and as was normal within the Indian community at the time, I was introduced to the daughter of a family friend as a potential wife. We met each other, got to know one another and agreed that we would get married. We got married about a year and a half later. I had a job I loved. Life was good.

About five years later we decided to start a family and had two children within three years. Life with the kids was great, but after the birth of the second, we started to have problems in our marriage. She suffered from post-natal depression, but denied it. I tried to be supportive but was pushed away and blamed for everything. Despite being a great dad, I was losing fast my ability to be a good husband. As these difficulties developed within my relationship, my longing for men started oozing out slowly. Having separate bedrooms allowed me to develop friendships with gay people online, giving me the confidence to start exploring my sexuality by talking to people. The more I developed these online 'relationships', the more I realised I was a gay man, but I couldn't say it. I could think it, but I couldn't say it. A million questions engulfed my mind: What would everyone think? I would lose my children, I would lose my family, everyone will be judging me, and so on and so forth.

By this stage, my marriage was over and we were two people bringing up children together and sharing a home and life, but we had grown so far apart that the gulf was too wide to build a bridge to go back to what we had.

Next, something would happen that would allow me to accept myself as a gay man. One of my online friendships was different to most others. It wasn't just about sex and other things of interest, but there was an amazing emotional connection. I was addicted, I was hooked, and I couldn't wait to meet him. He lived in Switzerland. He was a white European Swiss man who had converted to Islam at a young age. Given the negativity in the press about converts to Islam, I was nervous, but the emotional connection was too strong to resist. When we met for the first time, I felt like he held a key that had unlocked a whole new side to me. I was with him for the weekend and absolutely smitten and in love like I had never known before. I was in awe of his confidence not only in his sexuality, but also his faith. He could confidently be a gay Muslim man, despite harsh interpretations of the Islamic scripts in this regard. He knew no Muslims at the time of his draw to the faith, and his faith was so strong. I was in awe of his ability to be a 'White European Gay Muslim' man. He didn't care what anybody else thought. He lived his own life.

I realised I had embarked on a path from which there was no turning back. These feelings of love I felt for him were so overwhelming and made me feel so good, it was like nothing I had known before. Yes, I had loved my wife, but I hadn't ever experienced a love like this. I felt like I was a teenager again, but I wasn't, I had just turned thirty.

Now I had to contend with my sexuality, and one of the biggest eye-openers for me was that being gay or bisexual wasn't just about sex, but that it could be about love too. This was not something that I had thought of before. Furthermore, there was no reason why I couldn't maintain my identity as a Sikh man with a turban and be gay, although I had never seen a gay Asian, let alone a gay Sikh. The next steps inevitably involved some counselling, to try to confront my feelings for this man, which in turn led me to confront my sexuality. I remember crying with the counsellor about my fears, about these feelings, and she just smiled and said I should be happy that I was in love. I sat there and said to the counsellor, 'I am gay,' and to my amazement it made me feel good.

At this time there was more awareness of gay people. Gay rights were moving forward with not just discussions about equalities for gay people, but actual legislative proposals as well as there was talk of civil partnerships akin to marriage for gay people.

With this more positive environment developing, I needed to tell someone. I couldn't tell just anyone, though, and this was the next question that reverberated through me. The first non-gay person I had told about my sexuality was the counsellor. I remember the good feeling of being liberated when I told her that I was in love with a man, and she smiled back at me and said that was wonderful. There was no judgement, which was what I had expected. There was no ridicule, no shock horror. All these things I had expected. She was happy for me, so I felt I needed to tell someone else.

Interestingly at this time, a very close friend of mine had come out to me. His need to do this was because he had met someone and was now in a relationship. This boosted my confidence, and when he told me, I then told him I had also been in love with a man. His indifference to my 'announcement' gave me renewed vigour, though I was ever conscious that this was one of the hardest moments of my life. Telling someone would mean eventually having to break it to my wife (only in legal terms now, as we had, for some time, not had a sexual relationship) and eventually to tell my children. I felt mortified at the thought of telling my wife. I didn't want to break this bombshell to her, but I owed it to her to be honest. I had to test the water with someone close first who would not judge me, and the first person I told was my sister.

We had always been close, although I perceived her as a homophobe because she would always make negative remarks if she saw same-sex kissing or hugging on television, but I trusted her enough to tell her. So I did, and to my amazement she was also indifferent although surprised that I was married to a woman. We talked about my fear of losing my kids and other relationships, and she was amazingly supportive. I remember this being a rare occasion when I actually cried. I never cried, but I was crying at this moment. It was a huge sense of relief. Slowly after a comforting and heartfelt talk with my sister about my sexuality, I was more comfortable sharing my feelings with other people close to me in my life, though I was ever conscious of not telling anyone who knew my wife or came into contact with her.

Finally, I decided the time had come when I had to tell her. The question was, how would I do it? I had to consider several aspects to this 'coming out'. How did I support her to understand that the love we had was real and she had no part to play in me identifying myself in this way? How did we then decide whether we should tell the children? Do they need to know? How would we live our lives in the future given that we had children together and we couldn't just walk away from each other? I didn't want to do that anyway. I had loved this woman from the bottom of my heart at one point. I wanted to retain her friendship in my life. It took me the best part of two years to work out how to do it. I organised a family holiday for my wife and my kids, which in itself was not unusual. As was normal, we would split our bedrooms and have one child each in our rooms. The children were in a kids' club, enabling my wife and me to have some time alone. I had warmed her up to the fact that we should have some relationship discussions whilst the kids were in their club and we had time alone, and it would be nice to do it in a relaxed environment whilst we were on holiday.

So on holiday in the Mediterranean, the sun was shining, blue skies and beautiful relaxing scenery, we used this opportunity to talk and discuss our relationship. During these discussions, I came out to her. In the following days, there was anger, disbelief, understanding, reflections, denial. It was a very topsy-turvy range of emotions. I tried to reassure her that the love we had was true and still there, although now more as friendship rather than lovers. I wanted us to be friends who would bring up our children together. I wanted to provide her with the support to be able to come to terms with this. I felt incredibly sorry for putting her in such a position, but now I was aware I had to be honest with her. It was the right thing to do. These discussions were a roller coaster, but we agreed we had to focus on our children. She also told me she wouldn't accept me having a same-sex partner. Eventually, we had to agree to just focus on the children and other things one step at a time.

Life carried on, and as it did so, I had a few boyfriends with whom I had a variety of experiences of self-discovery. They all taught me things about myself, and each provided me with various degrees of confidence in myself as a gay man. All three of these men were amazing in differing ways, but for one reason or another, things didn't work out, and the common denominator seemed to be my marriage and children. This led me down the road to divorce and eventual separation from my children, by a former, now scorned, wife. She had gone out and told everyone about my sexuality, betraying my trust and forming very negative thoughts about me in people's minds. This led me to retreating back into defensive mode, because she had publicly outed me. This betrayal was too much for me to bear and took me down a self-destructive path, which required further counselling and a rebuilding of my life from the foundations up. I decided I wanted to take control and came across an inspiring Life Coach who provided me with some valuable insights into myself, along with a boost to my self-confidence, to help me stand up again, be tall and proud. I have not done anything wrong by being honest with those around me. I will not hide who I am again. I have come to accept that I do not require other people's validation or approval of me. I need to find the authentic me and be able to embrace this character and be proud of myself.

Part of this discovery involved me trying to discover the Sikh view on homosexuality. Could I be both Sikh and gay? The Sikh community are generally a conservative lot, which stems from their Indian cultural roots and origins. There was no talk of gay people in the community, not like mixed marriages, which as a child I remember caused a lot of problems, but since the nineties have become much more acceptable and tolerated. There was very little information available on homosexuality in Sikhism. I knew the views of homosexuality in other faiths, and it was again not a positive message. Eventually, I went to the basics of the faith. Guru Nanak Dev Ji, the founder of Sikhism, promoted equality between all people and love for all, all created by God and part of God. One of the Sikh prayers that all Sikhs recite daily invokes Sikhs to pray to the Almighty for the well-being of all humanity, prosperity for everyone in the worldwide community, and global peace for the entire planet. This is a clear indication that Sikhism accepts all people, including people of all sexual orientations and walks of life. Since this time, Sikh support groups have sprung up online. Sikhs now appear proudly wearing turbans at Gay Prides, so gay Sikh people are becoming more visible.

There are new challenges I am discovering, such as racism in the gay community. Despite there being no mention of homosexuality in Sikhism, there are a variety of views on whether it should be accepted or not within the Sikh faith, but in general there is virtually no discussion on the subject.

In order to make a difference and take some positive steps, I now volunteer for a charity called Diversity

Role Models, who run workshops in schools to tackle homophobia and challenge prejudice. As part of this work, I am proud to be a gay Sikh professional, and father too.

Anti-gay Countries of the World

There are 195 countries in the world, 81 of which have laws against homosexuals and homosexual activity, which means that 41 per cent of the world's population are living under laws that positively discriminate against homosexuality. There are 7.125 billion people in the world. If we use the rough conservative figure of 1.5 per cent of people being gay, this would equate to approximately 44,000,000 gay people living under regimes and in societies that are at best negative towards homosexuality and at worst where it is a punishable crime.

This list contains the 81 countries which uphold anti-gay laws:

>Afghanistan, Algeria, Angola, Antigua
>Bangladesh, Barbados, Belize, Bhutan, Botswana, Brunei, Burundi
>Cameroon, Comoros, Cook Islands
>Dominica (but no enforcement of anti-gay law)
>Egypt, Eritrea, Ethiopia
>Gambia, Ghana, Grenada, Guinea, Guyana
>India, Indonesia, Iran, Iraq

Jamaica

Kenya, Kirbati, Kuwait

Lebanon, Liberia, Libya

Malawi (enforcement of law suspended), Malaysia, Maldives, Mauritania, Mauritius, Morocco, Myanmar (Burma)

Namibia, Nauru, Nigeria

Oman

Pakistan, Palestine/Gaza, Papua New Guinea

Qatar

Samoa, Saudi Arabia, Senegal, Seychelles (Seychelles does not prosecute anyone under their anti-sodomy law and has promised to repeal it), Sierra Leone, Singapore, Solomon Islands, Somalia, South Sudan, Sri Lanka, St Kitts & Nevis, St Lucia, St Vincent & the Grenadines, Sudan, Swaziland, Syria

Tanzania, Togo, Tonga, Trinidad & Tobago, Tunisia, Turkmenistan, Tuvalu

Uganda, United Arab Emirates, Uzbekistan

Yemen

Zambia, Zimbabwe

Europe

No country in Europe has a law against homosexuality. The last European location with such a law was Northern Cyprus, which repealed that law in January 2014.

Also in Europe and worth mentioning, but not on the list of countries with laws against homosexuality are:

- Russia, which enacted an anti-gay propaganda law in 2013 prohibiting any positive mention of homosexuality in the presence of minors, including online
- Lithuania, which has a similar law
- Ukraine, which has considered but so far has not adopted a similar law against 'gay propaganda'
- Moldova, which adopted and then repealed such a law in 2013

It is worth noting also that some of the 81 countries in the list are more democratic and liberal than many of the others, and while their laws still uphold homosexuality as illegal, homosexual encounters still occur often in an illicit underworld environment. Many of the countries on the list, of course, have extreme laws against homosexuality.

For a comprehensive and up to date list of those countries with anti-gay laws go to:

http://www.bbc.co.uk/news/world-25927595

Here you will find a world map that shows which countries enforce the death penalty, imprisonment, have different ages for consent, laws against expression of homosexuality, and where marriage between same sexes is legal.

This is Edward's Story

I came out to my wife almost three years ago. It was the most difficult and painful thing I've ever had to do, but my story has a positive ending. The journey that led me to that moment will be familiar to many.

We met when we were teenagers, I was captivated by her and immediately fell head over heels in love. She was my first and only girlfriend. We were inseparable, best friends attacking life head-on. I was in a rush to make something of my life, and so the wedding and two children quickly followed. But I harboured a secret. It's amazing looking back that I managed to suppress my feelings for so long. Despite the signs being there from a very early age, I rationalised my desires as being a symptom of a high sex drive and someone who was just 'attracted to people'. The fact that I was fascinated by the men's underwear section in my mum's shopping catalogue at the age of twelve, or that I would regularly have explicit dreams about men and that I didn't seem to find any other woman on the planet sexually attractive were something I swept under the carpet. I spent my twenties with my head in the sand. Sex, love and having children were all boxes I'd ticked, so I focused on work, work, work.

In my early thirties as social media hit full force, I started to follow and befriend interesting people online. Many of these people were openly gay and I naturally started to gravitate towards them. I also started reading LGBT articles these people would post online, albeit terrified that someone would be reading over my shoulder. My porn-watching habits also changed. No longer could I keep pretending that I was remotely interested in the woman in the scene; in fact, I had dispensed of the women entirely. As I started to become more aware of my sexuality, I became more withdrawn. I had no friends, which was a situation entirely engineered by me so that I wouldn't be confronted by any awkward questions. A few times over the years I have been questioned over my sexuality. My reactions were always of acute embarrassment – think mini panic attack – which I felt gave some inner secret away. So I avoided any kind of personal relationships outside my marriage.

Then, in my mid-thirties, I met someone. It was by chance at a networking event for work, but there was an immediate spark. He was wonderful, confident in his own skin, and very interested in me. I'd never been able to make male friends easily, but here was someone just like me. After meeting him several times, I had that lightning-bolt moment where I finally 'came out' to myself as a gay man. I cried for the first time in years. A few months later, having sunk into the depths of depression, I told my wife.

For the next twelve months we went backward and forward over what to do. Her initial shock, anger, sadness and embarrassment faded. At points we ignored it, and at others we went through counselling, both as individuals and as a couple. Ultimately, she was looking to me for answers. I finally realised that nobody was going to come and save me from my situation. Only I could create my own future, and I just needed to decide what that future should look like. It dawned on me that I was being selfish by stringing things along, so I made the agonising decision that our marriage was over, but with a determination that our friendship and our family would go on.

After a year of uncertainty, I moved out into a rented flat Monday to Friday, while I was back in the family home at weekends. I used this time to explore my feelings and 'be sure', or as sure as I could be. The relationship with the guy I had met before ended when I became depressed, so it became my mission to seek out new gay friends. I joined an LGBT networking club, which worked wonders for my self-esteem. I also set about coming out to everyone – starting with my immediate family, then hers. We talked it all through together and in most cases told people in a coordinated 'united front' fashion. Without exception, reactions were supportive, but some needed a bit of educating to understand that we both intended to stay best friends.

The assumption is of infidelity and a bitter break-up, but that couldn't have been further from the truth. We both worked extremely hard to make our new relationship work. Sometimes that involved pushing boundaries and talking about uncomfortable things. There were conversations about what I had enjoyed sexually in our relationship and what I was looking for now. There were also lots of questions about what it means to be gay and the gay 'lifestyle'. Most difficult for me was opening up about the type of men I was attracted to, which celebrities I fancied and how that differed from her list.

For the large part we made it through laughter, the way we always had done in the past. On a more serious note, we talked about finances, longer term living arrangements, and how all this would impact on the kids. One of my biggest concerns was for our son, who isn't so confident at school. I was, and am still, afraid of him being bullied because of me, and we often talk about how he is doing. Slowly but surely, we transitioned from husband and wife to being close friends with a common goal, to protect our family and build on, rather than dismantle, what we had already achieved together.

The odd days are still painful and sad. A song or a photograph can set me off, wishing for my old life back and the future that never came to be. But I don't regret what I've done, and the vast majority of the time I feel extremely positive and proud to be a gay man with a best friend and beautiful kids.

Guilt plays a big part in most people's journey coming out later in life, but somehow I learnt to forgive myself. It's okay to not understand who you are in your teens and twenties, and your thirties, forties, fifties and beyond, for that matter. We all mature at different rates and are partly a product of the cultures and situations we have lived through. It isn't a crime to change and evolve, and it doesn't devalue what we have experienced and created on the journey.

Now, my ex-wife and I go to the cinema together on best friend dates, I spend family dinners with her parents, her brothers and sisters still consider me one of their siblings, and we've made a habit of going on fun-packed family holidays once or twice a year. We are one big unique family. Most recently, we've been tackling dating. We know this is something that could unbalance our happy medium, so as always, we're taking it slow and talking it through. I come as a package, as does she, and we've been clear about that from the outset. Luckily, I've met someone amazing who understands this completely, and I know that if I try hard enough, it will work. It already is, my boyfriend is just a new addition to our unique and happy family.

This is Fred's Story

When I was a boy I wanted to be black. It seemed an ideal way of being exotic and mysterious, yet at the same time it would mean I would be accepted, even given that this was the 1970s. I didn't know then that my needing to be accepted as 'normal' was behind this reasoning, all I knew was that I was off kilter, that I didn't feel the same as everybody else around me seemed to. I knew I was different. I wanted to be different, but I didn't know how.

Being a teenager in the '70s was only a short step away from being in the war – you can ask my kids, to them it's history. But it really did feel like we were only spitting distance from the Battle of Britain. There were still bomb craters; war films were staple viewing on Sunday afternoons and at the box office too. In games that involved baddies, they were always German, and nobody wanted to be on that side. I remember, too, hearing the regular testing of the air-raid siren at the railway station. It used to whirr into action then lull away again after a few minutes leaving the air still and quiet for a while afterwards, as if we were all thinking 'what if'. This was at the time of the Cold War; the end of the world was coming, we all knew it, and it was just a matter of time before the USSR pressed the button.

And yet, after the flower power and so-called 'sexual revolution' of the sixties, and when the world's obliteration was on the horizon, still the only real homosexual anybody knew of was some old, make-up-wearing and pink-dyed haired eccentric called Quentin Crisp. Oh, the hoo-hah in 1975 after *The Naked Civil Servant* was aired. At school, I cringed, joining in with all the parental disgust that was vented via the children on the playground. Ziggy Stardust was one thing, but Quentin Crisp, what was he?

The acceptable alternatives provided by the BBC and ITV (only three channels back then) were excruciating parodies of men trying to be women – Larry Grayson, the character guises of Dick Emery, 'Ooh you are awful, but I like you'; Danny La Rue weirdly parading around a vaudeville stage in *The Good Ol' Days* in frocks and feathers; and Mr Humphries, 'I'm free!' in *Are You Being Served?* Honestly, these were the only role models of homosexuality we had back then, apart from David Bowie of course, and he was an alien! Nobody thought that homosexuals actually existed in everyday life. These characters on TV were just playing a game, they didn't mean it – it made people laugh. The only one who did mean it was Quentin, and to a small-town boy, he seemed very scary.

I first kissed a boy in the loos at junior school. I don't know how it came about, I think we were showing each other how to do it properly. I know I found it more exciting than any lessons on biology. I don't think we really thought it was queer what we were doing, but we knew we had to hide away in the loos to do it. On one of the couple of occasions, that's all, the teacher came in and we froze in the cubicle. My pal climbed up onto the loo seat and I stood there so that if the teacher looked under the door, he'd only see one pair of legs. He must have known we were together in there, though, but maybe nothing in his teacher training at that time gave him the practicalities of how to deal with two frisky prepubescent boys locked in close quarters by the lips – there were no tongues. He left after a few moments, and we scarpered too. I don't suppose we ever had the nerve to repeat it after that.

Another time in the summer, whilst waiting for our turns to bat in the cricket match, three of us got our willys out and poked bits of straw into our urethras – you would have thought that would have been painful, but I must have enjoyed it because I can distinctly remember one boy being horrified that I had 'wee'd' myself. I hadn't, I was just excited, but I was mortified that he thought I'd wet myself. He and I weren't really friends, but funnily enough, years later he used to come and do a spot of gardening at our house, and I used to watch him from my brother's bedroom window with his shirt off and his chest hair stuck to his muscled torso with sweat. He was short but perfectly built, and he knew it. Roll on another year or two and I even went out with him one night on a sort of blind date with two gay hairdresser friends. I drove him home at the end of the night, but there wasn't any question of me pouncing on him. Why not? What a wasted moment that was. I was behaving – I think we were all behaving like this at that time – as if we weren't really interested in men, but it was sort of beguiling to give the impression that it was okay for some people, but not for us – not for me, anyway – that was just a step too far, and none of us were brave enough to take it.

There was something even more unusual, though, and perhaps more acceptable, something called 'bisexuality'. At a party I went to with my brother and cousin when I was about fourteen or fifteen, there was someone there openly calling himself bisexual. My brother would have been sixteen and my cousin fifteen, so there was lots of booze, cigarettes and older teenagers getting off with each other. Somehow I managed to get outside with this bisexual lad. He was, I suppose, in his late teens – he seemed very grown-up to me – and he seemed so glamorous labelling himself as 'bi', and yet so ordinary in his outward appearance. He was not effeminate in any way. Was this someone I could identify with? Was this what I was, a bisexual? At that age, I guessed it was. It seemed better than being associated with John Inman and the like. This guy was just your run-of-the-mill, jean-wearing, booze-swilling, cigarette- smoking bloke. We kissed – deeply, with tongues this time. It was everything I wanted and I wanted him to hold me and love me. I wanted to lie down on the damp grass with him, but he wouldn't, he knew I was too young. My brother and cousin came and 'rescued' me from his clutches, though I didn't want rescuing at all, and I couldn't stop thinking about him for days after, how I could set up a scenario where I could bump into him – but I never saw him again. The next day my brother asked me what I was doing. I said 'nothing'. I was so drunk I could get away with feigning having absolutely no knowledge of what had happened under the moonlight with ... what was his name? And I learned a quick lesson in survival – people will believe what you tell them, as long as you say it with conviction and believe in it yourself.

When I was eligible to drink, I discovered that the public toilets in the car park behind our local pub was a thriving 'cottage'. So one Monday evening, when I knew none of my mates would be out, I sat in the window of the pub and watched the cars come and go, all with single men of differing ages. I walked through the car park to another pub in town and nonchalantly popped in to the toilets on the way and found a guy at the urinal, but I didn't stop. What if he wasn't doing what I thought he was? What if it was some kind of set-up? So I to'd and fro'd from one pub to the other, popping in and out of the toilets on each circuit, and each time there would be someone in there and something going on, but I didn't feel party to it, more like I was gate-crashing.

As darkness fell and I got more and more drunk and more daring with each passing swing-by, someone finally spoke to me as I hung about outside. He asked me what I was looking for. I didn't know what he meant, this was all new to me, and I didn't have the words to convey how horny I felt and that anything from a grope to a blow job would have been enough to satisfy my urges. Fortunately, he could see how I was floundering. It didn't take a detective to work it out. We arranged to meet later at a bus stop and he suggested we go somewhere quieter, which turned out to be another public toilet in a smaller town five miles down the road. Anyway, I went with him. Anything could have happened, of course, but danger is a foreign land when you're young and drunk. He was a bit older than me, maybe in his early twenties. I remember he asked me my age, and I lied and told him I was 'twenty, nearly twenty-one', because the legal age back then was twenty-one, but he didn't believe me. I was, in fact, only eighteen, nearly nineteen, because I remember it was the summer and it was a warm and balmy night. All we did in the tight space of the toilet cubicle was kiss and give each other a handjob, but just holding a man close to me and tightly was manna from heaven.

The toilets behind the pub and the car park became my after-hours regular haunt. Once the pubs kicked out at 10.30pm or 11pm at the weekend, I would wander homewards with my mates then secretly double back on myself once we had parted company. Each night, after the pubs had closed, I patrolled the town like a fox waiting for men to come out. I loved and hated what I was doing. It was addictive, and each time, I thought, this would be the one. I remember one guy who was really good-looking, dark and handsome, who'd gone to the Chinese to get a takeaway for him and his missus on the way home, and stopped off at the cottage toilets with his brown paper bag of sweet and sour, which he popped down on the ground while we frantically groped at each other. These liaisons were invariably over in minutes. If I thought about it now hard enough, I'm sure I could remember more occasions, like the time I got in a car and went back to this guy's flat. I was so drunk I threw up in his toilet before lying on his bed with him.

I remember we were always very careful. This was at a time when it was not only criminal, importuning and having sex in public, but it was the beginning of the eighties and the scourge of AIDS was starting to take its grip. I remember talking about it in the pub with my circle of friends, both boys and girls, and me loudly saying how any one of us could be contaminated with this terrible disease, but they still didn't get what I was actually implying.

I was living a dual existence, and no one seemed to notice. By day I worked and had a girlfriend; in fact, I had one or two, one after the other, but they would want commitment and love, so I would end it. I socialised with a wide group of mates, but by night I was a predatory homo discovering all the best places to hook up – the toilets, the park, and now driving to further afield places like nightclubs, but always at times when I couldn't be found out. Occasionally, I took myself off to London for weekends, staying with friends who had made the move there in search of work. I would always take the opportunity to visit a cinema or strip joint in Soho before I arrived on their doorsteps. A couple of times I went to Heaven and bumped into Freddie Mercury once, and he gave me the eye – how lucky was I – a narrow escape. At a nightclub in the nearest city to where I lived, they ran a gay-night on Wednesdays. This was perfect because none of my circle of friends went out during the week, so Grannies became another regular pickup joint for me, or for me to be picked up. Even inside a gay disco I was still wary and scared to talk to guys first. I would sit there in a cubicle, looking erudite and sophisticated, and wait for someone to slide up next to me and start talking. These were the guys I should have been hanging out with and going to parties with, of course, instead of my straight mates down the pub. These guys were young, good-looking and looking for love, just like me, but I only ever went on one-night stands. They were still all too queer for my liking, except one married guy who I saw a couple of times and went back to his hotel. He wouldn't ever tell me his story, just that he was some kind of architect and that he worked away from home sometimes. I hadn't a clue then, but I figure now he must have had a wife and kids at home.

Once, at the nightclub, my mum's hairdresser was there, and I asked him not to say anything to her. Of course he did, he couldn't help himself. I'm sure he thought he was only trying to help me out, but it came up at the following Sunday lunch when my then girlfriend was there too. 'Graham said he saw you the other night at Grannies,' my mum enquired in all innocence, until she made the ubiquitous Dick Emery flick-of-her-wrist gesture that spelled out all too clearly to everyone what that place was and that it was frequented by poofters. I looked at my girlfriend and my brother and my mum and said quite coolly, 'Oh, it's one of these new "radical" one-nighters they occasionally have on.'

My girlfriend didn't seem fazed by the news and, in fact, came along with me the following week. This was the age of the New Romantics, and the gay night at the club attracted all sorts: girls and boys. I did finally confess to her that I like boys as well as girls on a trip to Paris – that I was bisexual. But that wasn't really the truth. I was behaving like a depraved con artist. Is that too strong a simile? I was a manipulator of the truth to the point that I convinced myself wholeheartedly that this was all okay, that a dual life, one carried on in the glitzy darkness and one in daylight, was perfectly manageable. What I was doing of course, was searching desperately for someone to love, but in completely all the wrong places. I knew I was not a screaming queen, I was just a young guy who liked men's bodies, and nobody seemed to notice this about me. My mum never mentioned it again, my circle of friends never said anything either, not even when I shared the back of a van at a rock festival with one and he caught me masturbating in the morning. I wanted him to catch me, of course, and I wanted him to join in, but he just turned over. Nor did my mate who used to stay over and top and tail with me in my bed, while I spent half the night fidgeting. He was one of the ones I stayed with in London and he told me, in no uncertain terms, when we shared his bed in his tiny bedsit, that there was to be 'no funny business'. I made out I hadn't a clue what he was talking about. My disguises worked every time. I don't think I saw him again after that weekend, though. My hopes of ever getting into his pants were dashed, you see, so I dropped him.

  I knew I had to get away from my small-town life if I was ever to meet anyone and have a relationship. Although I don't think I actually considered ever living with a guy or having a boyfriend as a feasible possibility. Did young guys actually do that other than rent-boys in Soho and rich public school boys on the Grand Tour, like in *Brideshead Revisited*? I just wanted to meet like-minded people. I became infatuated with a boy who looked like Billy Idol. He was everything I longed for and wanted to be myself. He had a girlfriend but was obviously toying with gender-bending, as we called it back then. Somehow we had the conversation. I'm sure it was all done in code, unsaid innuendo and supposition, but he said that had we met a few years earlier, before his girlfriend came along, we could have given it a go, but as it was, it wasn't going to happen. I've never got over him, and there's always been that 'what if' in the back of my mind whenever I think about him. I wonder what he's doing now?

After that I left my job and went to Europe for a while and got some seasonal work on a farm. There were lots of young people there my age, but no one was bent like me. I felt like a tiny, insignificant minority in what was a normal world to everyone else. I was always on the outside looking in on something I couldn't quite relate to. Like being at a party where you don't know anyone. After the season finished on the farm, I came home from France very ill, to the point where I could have died, and of course, I'm sure everybody was thinking the same as me, that it might have been AIDS, but in fact, it was some awful viral disease that attacked my muscles. It took me several months to get back to full health and fitness again, and when I did, I landed a job working in a restaurant. This was where I met the girl who was to be my wife.

The transient world of restaurant work was the ideal situation for me; I could now lead three lives. I saw my mates less frequently and now built up a new circle of well-travelled, worldly people who were working at the restaurant between other fabulous adventures – mostly dreams, truth be known. So here I could be legitimately attracted to men while the girls clamoured around me because I was slightly older than the others and they quite liked the idea of taming a bisexual man. There was one girl in particular, and we hit it off immediately. Nothing seemed impossible for us. We quickly became boyfriend and girlfriend and moved into a shared house with some of the others, and we had a ball, partying and thinking ourselves terribly glamourous. When I went home to my other life, I became one of the lads again and would do the late-night circuit, prowling the streets for a bit of action, just like the old days. It was a whirl of a time and we had a blast in those few years in the mid-eighties. I seemed to be free, stepping in and out of people's lives with a whole wardrobe of clothes befitting the personality, I thought, they thought they knew.

My love, for that's what she became, flew to Canada to spend some time travelling around with some girlfriends. While she was gone, I took myself off to an island in the Med and had another one-night stand with a boy who seemed to be on the same journey as me. He was desperately scared of who he was, what he was becoming, of catching AIDS and what his father would say if he found out about him. I could have loved that boy, but he slipped away before I knew it. Meantime, I missed my girlfriend, I mean I really missed her – I was in love. We both were, and when she returned from her travels, we moved to London together to start a new life. We both landed decent jobs, bought a small flat, and a couple of years later got married. It was the next step in our relationship, it wasn't planned or a whirlwind romance, it just developed that way, and I couldn't imagine living the rest of my life with anyone else. Of course, she knew about my sexual dalliances in the past, but it was never spoken about and I carried on believing that that side of my life had nothing to do with my relationship with my then wife, or indeed the rest of the world. So much so, that even on the eve of my wedding I visited a sauna in London for one last go – of course it wasn't, and so I began down the road of treachery, using every opportunity to my advantage. When she was away or after we moved back down south, every time I had to visit the London office through work, I would always finish the day with a visit to the sauna.

This was all fine and never impacted on our lives at home until the birth of our first son and we made the decision that it would be me who stayed at home to look after him and my wife would go back to work. Even then this was quite unusual and I hadn't bargained for feeling so isolated and alone – something I think a lot of women also find who give up a career to look after their children. Gay sex dried up; there were simply never any opportunities. Our own sex life was becoming less and less frequent and more and more clinical. We were doing it because we felt we had to. During the pregnancy of our second child, my wife discovered something I had downloaded on the computer. This was in the early days of the home PC and I was slowly discovering the world of gay porn that was starting to get a grip on the dial-up Internet. I had downloaded some pictures – just beautiful guys, not pornographic or anything, but I'd also found a blog written by a gay married man in America, and I'd replied to it and saved a copy. She rang me at work in tears, and I made out to my work colleagues that she thought she was going into labour. When I got home, there were a lot more tears, but an almost total lack of emotion from me. I was so able to completely distance myself from that other life that it was almost as if it was somebody else we were talking about.

We patched things up. I carried on as if nothing had changed, but for her the whole world was now a different place. Our second son was born and she went back to work and started to build her own life outside the family home. She was doing what I had done for so many years, but whereas I had never let it impact on our lives until that day I 'left' the stuff on the computer (and I do believe I subconsciously did that on purpose because I wanted her to find it and there to be some resolution to my situation), she started an affair and started staying out overnight and even talking on her phone in the house to her boyfriend, whom she said was also living in a very difficult situation with a wife he no longer loved or was having a relationship with. It was very hard for him, she said. She couldn't see how he was using her, and I watched as over the months the inevitable happened and the affair came to an end. All the while I carried on looking after the children and the house and doing my duty. I swore I would never leave them.

In the end, she could take it no more and decided to leave the family home and start a new life for herself. She was very lucky to be able to do that, buying her own home whilst still contributing to the boys' upbringing and their home and mine. We had basically completely swapped roles; she took the role of the man, having an affair and leaving, and I was the wife, working part time and trying to keep everything together for our sons. Of course, I was now free and living in a nice house, but it was only ever temporary until the boys left school, and I couldn't go out of an evening because I couldn't leave them, and I didn't want to face the questions about where I was going and with whom. So I was living a celibate life by this stage. Porn became my boyfriend.

Finally, the demand for divorce came, and then everything really changed. She wanted her share of the equity out of the house; so I had to sell despite my lawyer saying that she would fight for me to stay in the family home for as long as my youngest son was still at school, but it all got very messy and emotional, so I agreed to sell, and negotiated a settlement better than that which my wife wanted. She said it was all my fault and why should she have to lose out. It wasn't my 'fault', I couldn't help it, and I never let it impinge on our lives together, until that one day when I left that stuff on the computer. I think it was either that or I would have slowly gone into meltdown. I think I subconsciously saved myself.

Since the divorce I have moved into a very nice rented apartment with my youngest son. I have much more 'me' time now that he is older, and I am starting to build a life I should have had thirty years ago. The only trouble is, most of the gay men my age are now in couples, so it's very difficult to meet anyone. Thank heavens for Internet dating, although that's not been a success yet, and the GADS, without whom I would still feel very isolated. It's taken me forty-five years to realise that other men like kissing men too, that they played with dolls when they were little, and they wanted to be fathers and commit to all the responsibilities that brings.

Thank God we live in a different age where tolerance of an individual's sexuality is the norm. Britain leads the way in this, because it is in our nature to be tolerant of others. I wish we'd had the Internet when I was a teenager. It seems all so much easier now for the young to hook up with like-minded people. It was impossible in 1976. I regret I didn't trust of few more guys I met along the way and opened up to them, but fear of rejection and ridicule are very strong forces to deal with. Slowly, I am getting a grip, and in my mid-fifties, with the support of dear, life-long friends who haven't batted an eyelid when I've told them, I am at least enjoying my new found freedom, and who knows, one day I might meet someone special.

Criminal Law

Henry VIII introduced the first legislation against sodomy in England under English criminal law with the Buggery Act of 1533, making buggery punishable by hanging. A penalty not lifted until 1861. Until the passing of the Act, all sexual activities except adultery were ignored. The Act itself states that the only reason for implementing it was because before that there was 'no sufficient punishment'. The Act, which made buggery with a man or beast equally punishable, was piloted through Parliament by Thomas Cromwell, Henry's favoured minister at the time, and it is suggested, though there is no evidence of this, that the Act was introduced as a measure against the clergy, as it quickly followed the separation of the Church of England from Rome.

Contravention of the Act, along with treason, led Walter Hungerford, 1st Baron Hungerford of Heytesbury, to become the first person to be executed under the statute in July 1540, though it was probably the treason that cost him his life. Nicholas Udall, a cleric, playwright, and Headmaster of Eton College, was the first to be charged for violation of the Act alone, in 1541. In his case the sentence was commuted to imprisonment, and he was released in less than a year.

'Classic' charges brought against gay men engaging in consensual sexual offences are buggery, gross indecency and importuning ('to persistently solicit or importune in a public place for immoral purposes'). Most of the prosecutions under these laws were on men caught allegedly abusing the facilities of public lavatories (cottages) or engaging in sexual activity at night in deserted parks or wasteland (cruising grounds).

Despite publicity about the removal of laws relating to 'cottaging', a specific offence of 'sex in a public toilet' has been introduced. The new offence carries a sentence of up to six months in prison.

From 1 May 2004, under the Sexual Offences Act 2003, some men, convicted in the past of consensual sex with a young man aged sixteen or seventeen, remain on the sex offenders' register for activity which is either no longer a crime, or, if it is, no longer triggers the registration requirement. These men can now apply to be removed from the register and should be informed by letter by the police of their right to do so.

Cottages/cottaging

'Cottaging' is a UK gay slang term that has become exclusively used when referring to anonymous sex between men in a public lavatory, a 'cottage', or 'tea room' (the American slang equivalent), and/or cruising for sexual partners with the intention of having sex elsewhere. The term has its roots in self-contained English toilet blocks resembling small cottages in their appearance and often hidden away among trees in corners of parks. The term is documented as having been in use during Victorian times.

Cottages were among the few places where gay men and those too young or too afraid to go into a gay bar could meet other men for casual sex. Cottages are located in places used by many people, such as bus stations, railway stations, airports and university campuses. Glory holes are sometimes drilled in the walls between cubicles in popular cottages, and under-stall foot signals are used to signify the wishes of one man to connect with the person in the next cubicle.

Since the 1980s authorities have become increasingly more aware of the existence of cottages in their areas and in some, have reduced the height of or even removed doors from the cubicles, or extended the walls between the cubicles to the floor. Sexual acts in public lavatories are outlawed by many councils, but it is precisely the element of risk involved in cottaging that makes it exciting.

The Internet is transforming cottaging, and there's a large online community in which men exchange details of locations, discuss aspects such as which 'cottage' or cruising spot receives the highest traffic, whether it is safe, how much it is used by the general public and so on, and also to facilitate meeting times.

Historically in the UK, gay sex in a public place resulted in a charge of gross indecency. The Sexual Offences Act 1967 permitted homosexual sex between consenting adults over the age of twenty-one years when conducted in private. The act specifically excluded public lavatories from being 'private'. The Sexual Offences Act 2003 eventually removed this contentious offence in favour of 'indecent exposure'. According to a BBC report in October 2008: 'People caught having sex in public should only be arrested as a last resort, according to draft police guidelines.'

In many of the cases where men are brought to court for cottaging, the issue of entrapment arises. Since the offences are public, but often carried out behind closed doors, the police have sometimes used undercover police officers posing as homosexuals to frequent known cottages in an effort to entice other men to approach them for sex – the classic 'honey-trap'. These men would be arrested for indecent assault, but such practices by the police have been curtailed after a judge in one case decided that a police officer had consented to such an assault, because he required the defendant to touch him with sexual intent in order to have the evidence that a crime had been committed. Alternatively, an arrest could be issued for importuning, which requires a much lower burden of proof and comes with a shorter maximum sentence.

There have been many cases of celebrities, famous politicians and members of the aristocracy who have been arrested for cottaging over the years. Actor John Gielgud was arrested in 1953 and fined £10 for importuning. The famous court case was later made into a play *Plague Over England* by Nicholas de Jongh, which had a successful West End run when it premiered there in 2008.

Wilfrid Brambell, who played Steptoe in the hit 1960s TV show, was arrested in a public toilet in Shepherd's Bush in 1962. Whilst in New York in the same year, the Mansfield Police Department conducted a sting operation in which they covertly filmed men having sex in a public restroom underneath Central Park. Thirty-eight men were convicted and jailed for sodomy. After the arrests, the city closed the restrooms and the police later made the film footage they had secretly obtained into a training film. It was rereleased in 2007 and called *Tearoom*.

In 1968 Michael Turnbull was arrested in a public toilet in Hull, before he became Bishop of Durham; and Peter Wyngarde, the actor who played Jason King in the TV detective series of the same name, was arrested in 1975 in Gloucester bus station's public toilets for gross indecency with a truck driver. He was fined £75. Even Coronation Street has not been without its share of 'cottagers' when in 1981, actor Peter Dudley, who played Bert Tilsley, was observed exposing himself to another man in a public toilet in Didsbury, Manchester, and charged with importuning. He pleaded guilty and was fined £200. Some months later Dudley was charged again with gross indecency for an alleged similar offence, though this time he claimed he was not guilty and had been set up by the police. A Crown Court jury failed to reach a verdict, but while waiting for a retrial, Dudley suffered a series of strokes and heart attacks and died in October 1983.

Probably the most famous case of a celebrity being caught out in a public toilet was that of pop star George Michael in April 1998, who was arrested for 'engaging in a lewd act' in an LA restroom after a sting operation by the local police. Although Michael considered the arrest to be police entrapment, he pleaded 'no contest' to the charge in court and was fined $810 and ordered to do eighty hours of community service. Later that year the star satirised the events in his music video for the song 'Outside' and was sued by one of the officers in the original arrest for portraying him as non-heterosexual and mocking him. The suit was ultimately dismissed.

This is Grant's Story

I made a conscious choice at the age of twenty-four not to be gay. I persuaded myself that if I could still get it up with girls and have a good time with them, then I could be happy. Wrong! Oh so wrong. With a beautiful wife and two boys aged eleven and thirteen at the time, I was coming to a major crossroads in my life. My wife had known about me being gay for three years previously, as I was outed unintentionally by an SMS to her from a friend! Some of our friends knew too, but not the kids or our families.

My work takes me abroad a lot and Gaydar (the online dating site for gay men) is great for that, just hooking up, but what you cannot allow for is love. My wife and I were great friends, although it had its limits, of course, but I fell in love with men twice in three years and that's when the separation of sex abroad and family life at home doesn't work. We lived together as a couple, and when I was home, everything was still secretive, for the kids obviously, but also for her. I came to realise that what I wanted was a simpler, more honest life, but I wondered whether that was only ever going to be a delusion. Could I swap a stable yet happy and loveless home for an uncertain future of love and two homes? So many of my gay friends told me it wasn't worth it, but I hated what I was going through, so how could it be worse?

When I told my parents, they were fine about the separation to start with, but then the real reason hit the fan. I looked my mother straight in the eye and told her I was gay and she didn't bat an eyelid. Of course she knew, but I wasn't going to make things worse by drawing attention to this and making her feel guilty. Then she told me I had AIDS! Nice one, Mum! Dad tried to smooth things over, but all my mother saw was her own humiliation.

I told my eldest boy, who by then was fourteen, that his mum and I were separating, and initially he was angry. 'Why couldn't you do this when I was five or eighteen?' he shouted. 'Why do you have to separate just because the spark has gone between you two?' (Kids can be so observant). I hadn't told him that I was gay because I thought that by the time he was ready to find out, he'd know anyway. The day afterwards, I went back and we all had a group hug. That seemed to break the ice and he was fine after that. My ex-wife and I both instinctively knew that the secret with him was to show him that we were fine with it and we could still laugh. My mistake was not having a group of supportive friends. 'Our' friends were no good in this situation. At the beginning of my life as a single man I went for quantity not quality, but once things started stabilising, I redressed that balance. My relationship with my ex-wife was, for the most part, good with the occasional flare-up, but I bit my tongue and we managed to keep a lid on it.

Life got considerably better, and after a few months I had a circle of friends I could call on; I'd established a routine and bought a new place. I found a wonderful man too, who I adored, loved and cherished, and I could almost say that I had arrived at the place I was aiming for all those years, and that it had been worth it.

It's difficult to really know when normality re-established itself. It's not something that presents itself very clearly once you have achieved it, but looking at the dates, it must have been at the end of 2008. Since then a pattern has established itself and I have great relationships with my partner, my ex-wife, kids and friends. I found Steven quite by chance through an event held by an online group for gay dads. It was early on in the split from my wife, so both Steven and I were both quite wary of what was happening, but it has stood the test of time. We live an hour away by train and see each other at weekends, but he has visited me many times while I have been working abroad, and we've had quite a few holidays together. The important thing for me is that we share the goal of eventually living together. When that will be, neither of us can really predict. I have my ageing parents living in London and he still has a teenager living at home with his mum. So, for the moment, we are constrained by circumstance, but I could not want for a more loving, kind and gentle partner than Steven.

The relationship with my ex-wife is now really good. It helped enormously when she found someone else and had a relationship, which lasted about a year. We talk over her dates since then and all the ins-and-outs of her latest adventures. I will never be entirely at peace, I don't think, until she does find the right guy, but I'm happy when she is happy. We remain married, but live apart. I'm glad of that because it gives her financial security and keeps me involved in fixing things that go wrong (I'm quite good at fixing most things, except being gay).

We still take the kids on holiday and behave correctly as if we were still together as far as they are concerned. She and I did start 'Collaborative Divorce' proceedings, but it soon became apparent that the costs were escalating to the ruination of us both, so we stopped it. I'm glad we did start it, though, because she could see that I was not out to leave her high and dry, and she realised that the lawyers were actually taking money out of 'our' pot. An expensive lesson, but nevertheless worthwhile to prove that we were better at working out what was best for us without any outside help.

What gems of wisdom can I impart to any other dads coming out?

1. Prepare yourself financially. It's going to cost!
2. Make sure you have a good circle of friends to lean on.
3. If you move out, always rent. It may be a waste of money, but six months on you'll have a much better understanding of how your future will be.
4. Suffer the brickbats of recriminations. Behave correctly and in the end she will recognise that the man she married has not turned into a monster just because he's gay.
5. Give it time and hold off going to the lawyers until you both feel it is right to do so. Work it out before you go and it'll cost so much less.
6. If the kids see that you are both trying to work it out and that you are behaving correctly, they will toe the same line. This

works up to the age of seventeen or eighteen, after that it's more unpredictable, but separation these days is much less of an issue since there's so much of it about.

7. Don't get hung up too much on how the kids will react. They're more interested in whether they will have to sleep somewhere else. Your emotional life is not that interesting to them unless they're older than eighteen.

8. If you haven't explored your gay side while married, then get on with it. I know there are exceptions, but in general, the chances of a fifty-year-old man living the rest of his life with a thirty-year-old are few and far between. So run after the younger man for a while, but don't confuse love with infatuation.

This is Harry's Story

I was born in London into a very loving family, the firstborn son to carry on the family name with big expectations for me to marry and produce children. As it so happens I really did want to get married and become a father. I remember at school thinking how much I was attracted to both boys and girls, and that thanks to good genes I wasn't short of girlfriends, but I always knew something was missing.

I had my first experience with a guy when I was eighteen; he was twenty-five and took me away to Brighton for the weekend in his convertible. All I had to do was tell my parents, and girlfriend, that I was going away with some mates for a lads' weekend. That was the first time I slept with a man. It was a real turn-on, but I felt so nervous and worried someone would find out somehow. I wasn't ready for this, and if I thought about a full-on relationship with a man, it just seemed something impossible to me. I also really wanted to be a dad one day, so I put the weekend behind me and went back to my girlfriend.

When I was twenty-one and single again, I met my future wife. We fell madly in love, and by the age of twenty-six, we were married and planning a family. My first daughter was born in 2005 and I fell in love again. I did not imagine on my wedding day that I could live with a man, and when my children came along, that I could be separated from them.

My attraction to men was always there, though, and I was now working in the city with lots of professional guys around me and I met Marcus. I honestly didn't know where my life was going. I was drinking excessively to try to escape the guilt of cheating on my pregnant wife again, but Marcus was always there for me, supporting me any way he could.

In November 2006, just before our second daughter was born, I had a breakdown and got home really drunk. In all the outpouring and with so much guilt built up inside me, I came out to my wife. She was so strong and said, quite understandably, that she could not deal with it at that time, as she was just about to give birth. I fell into a black hole and ended up coming out to everyone because I knew she needed support. My guilt was so intense because it was all such bad timing, yet it was supposed to be a happy time. My second daughter was born and my wife did everything she could to keep me at home.

As I had finally come out as gay – although I now realise I am not completely gay, as I could still have a relationship with a woman, I just prefer a man's body – I left the family home just after Christmas 2006. I will never get that image out of my mind, of me leaving my wife and two babies on the doorstep as I walked away with a bin bag of clothes to the car, where Marcus was waiting to take me home to his place in south London.

Most of my friends and family could not deal with it, and my father didn't talk to me for two years. This whole period is a bit of a blur, as I was really all over the place while still trying to do my best to see my daughters and ensure that my wife was okay. She, of course, went through all the emotions, and the guilt was horrendous, but I knew I could not go back.

Things seemed to move very quickly after that, and Marcus and I were totally wrapped up in each other. He even sold his beautiful house in London to move to Hertfordshire so that I could be closer to my children. We all tried to adapt to the situation and get on with our lives. It was so tough for all of us and I only had Marcus for support. At that time, I did not have a support group to help me. I concentrated my time on being with my daughters as much as possible and working hard at my career, and my wife seemed to be doing better than me.

We divorced in 2007 and I carried on fully supporting her with the finances and children. When she met her now husband, things started to turn sour between her and I. No one will ever get in the way of me seeing my daughters, so we had a few strained years.

Marcus and I now live in a beautiful house, which we own together. My daughters are nearly eleven and nine, and are so great with him. Marcus and my ex-wife get on really well now – even having coffee together sometimes – I don't want to know what their conversations are about!

Would I do the same thing again? I really don't know, as it was so hard for everyone at first, and every day I still feel guilty for walking out on a lovely wife and two beautiful babies, but seeing how we are all happy now, it makes it a lot easier to bear. I wish I had had a support group back then. I have met some great gay dads who have become lifelong friends.

I think more needs to be discussed around the issues of sexuality in schools. My daughters, however, think it's really cool to have a gay dad, and all their girlfriends want to come and stay with us, which is great. I partly envy the new generation of gay dads. They have a great support network, but I don't envy having to go through all the emotional roller-coaster stuff that is inevitable.

You cannot deny your sexuality. I honestly would have preferred it if I had been completely heterosexual, as I think it's a much easier life, but I am lucky how things have turned out and that I have a very supportive partner, two beautiful daughters and a very supportive family. My father is now good friends with Marcus, and we have made a lot of new friends together, so life is finally starting to settle after so many years.

Where did the term *homosexual* originate?

'What is homosexuality?' seems to be a fairly straightforward question to ask in a modern, Western context, but it would not be answered the same the world over or if asked at different historical points in time. We would think of homosexuality as a clear-cut concept of sexual preference and identity based on some inherent biological predisposition. However, the word or term *homosexuality* was only invented in the nineteenth century and added to by the term *heterosexuality* later in the same century. The term *bisexuality* was invented in the twentieth century. Later, *transgender, pangender, asexual* and *LBGT* terms and others have been added as the variances in sexual behaviour and preferences have become more widely acknowledged.

There are no words in Latin that precisely translate to 'homosexuality' or 'heterosexuality', and in Roman times these concepts were unrecognisable.

The one person most responsible for the creation of the label *homosexual* was Karl Ulrichs (1825–95). Ulrichs, a German law student, secretary to various civil servants and diplomats, and a journalist, was not a medical doctor. In May 1862, an acquaintance of his was arrested for public indecency. As a result of this, Ulrichs, who was also known to be sexually attracted to men, decided to try to solve the 'riddle' of man-to-man love and sexual attraction.

In November of that year he began work on 'The Race of Uranian Hermaphrodites, The Man-Loving Half-Men'. He finished most of it in 1863 and published *Researches on the Riddle of Male-Male Love* in 1864 under the pseudonym Numa Numantius. By 1879 he had published twelve volumes on the subject.

Ulrichs's 'scientific' inspiration was contemporary embryology. It had been discovered that the sex organs are indistinguishable in the early stages of foetal development. By his analogy, homosexual desire was just as natural, and he believed that the 'germ' of the female sex could be retained in the fully developed male, creating a kind of psychic hermaphrodite – a half-man with a feminine sex drive within the male body. He came up with the phrase 'a feminine soul' to describe this.

The substantive source for Ulrichs's theory was not in medicine, but Plato's *Symposium*, in which Pausanius says that love for males is the offspring of Heavenly Love (Aphrodite Urania) who is the daughter of Uranus, and love for females is the offspring of Common Love (Aphrodite Pandeumia) the daughter of Zeus and Dione.

Ulrichs modified these terms in accordance with the German language and came up with the following:

Urning for homosexual male

Dioning for heterosexual male

Urningin for lesbian

Dioningin for heterosexual female

As Ulrichs became more widely acquainted with other homosexuals, he realized there were many variations and he expanded this in his classification system. But due to its complexities, this terminology was gradually dropped, although it lived on in England for almost half a century as 'Uranian love'. The system of descriptive classification used today is:

Homosexual: active/masculine or receptive/effeminate

Bisexual: closet or latent gay situational homosexual

The concept of the 'feminine soul' has been dropped since the 1960s, though in the 1990s it was revived in the term *transgender*. Many, perhaps most, folk cultures have a concept of a natural (biological) third sex in addition to male and female, and the most recent anthropological theorists are coming round to the possibility that there really is physiologically and psychologically a third sex or gender.

The word *Homosexualität* was coined by the German-Hungarian Károly Mária Kertbeny in the nineteenth century. It is a compound of the Greek *homo*, 'same', and Mediaeval Latin *sexualis*, 'sexual'. It occurs first in a letter from Kertbeny to Karl Ulrichs, dated 6 May 1868, and then in two pamphlets published in 1869 in Leipzig, arguing for the reform of the Prussian Penal Code, which was against sexual relations between men. The term was not used again until 1880, when a text written by Kertbeny was published in a popular-science book. Also at this time, the word *Heterosexualität* first appeared, taken from a paper by Kertbeny and attributed to 'Dr M'. Thus heterosexuals were invented eleven years later than homosexuals.

The pseudonym 'Dr M' helped to promote the belief that Kertbeny was a doctor or scientist, when in fact he was a writer. We know little about his life, though he seems to have died of syphilis. He claimed to be a *Normalsexualer*, but he spent so many years campaigning, either anonymously or using pseudonyms, that there are suspicions about his own homosexual tendencies.

Kertbeny invented the term *homosexuality* as part of an argument that it was natural and a matter of private behaviour that should be beyond the interference of the law.

He intended it to be used as a neutral, non-judicial term. It was devised precisely in order to serve the emancipationist needs of a network of gay-identified German men, who for a dozen years at least had been advocating the reform of laws against them and the education of society regarding their modes of behaviour.

The label *homosexual*, instead of being created by society to control people, was therefore, self-generated by gay (or gay-friendly) men to empower individuals and set them on the road to freedom rather than enslavement.

Ulrichs did claim to have discovered feminine traits within himself *after* he developed the third-sex theory: 'not everyone arrives at a consciousness of this female element. I myself became aware of it only very late, and I might never have arrived at it had I not pondered the riddle of Uranian love or become acquainted with other Urnings.' Even if this were true, the label nevertheless arose from within Ulrichs's struggle to solve a riddle about himself – it was not imposed by society in order to control him.

Ulrichs's theory that homosexuality was natural and congenital was later significantly modified in accordance with a criminal/medical model that emphasized perversion, sickness, and deficiency. Ulrichs summed this up: 'My scientific opponents are mostly doctors of the insane. They have observed Urnings in lunatic asylums and have apparently never seen mentally healthy Urnings. The published views of the doctors for the insane are now accepted by others.' Unfortunately, Ulrichs's term *half-man* easily fell within the view of homosexual men as being incomplete or defective.

Homosexualität, 'homosexuality', was a very useful neutral way to refer to 'same-sex love', which 'scientifically' defused such highly charged words as 'bugger' or 'sodomite'. But it was not taken up quickly enough by the scientific community of physicians and anthropologists.

The word *homosexual* did not appear in English until 1891, in John Addington Symonds's *A Problem in Modern Ethics* where he used the phrase 'homosexual instincts'. In *Sexual Inversion*, 1897, Havelock Ellis popularized the idea of 'inversion' as an inborn gender anomaly. Addington felt strongly that homosexuals should be considered as a 'minority' group, but gave way to Ellis's view of homosexuality as a neurosis and congenital abnormality in the hope, proven vain, that this would gain sympathy and tolerance from the general public.

Quoted with kind permission from Rictor Norton; *A Critique of Social Constructionism and Postmodern Queer Theory*, 'The Term "Homosexual"', 1 June 2002, updated 19 June 2008

http://rictornorton.co.uk/social14.htm

This is Ian's Story

Here it is – my first ever blog! Sunday 09 November 2008

Married twelve years, with an eight-year-old son; wife best friend for nearly twenty years and very supportive, but understandably upset since we seem to have drifted apart, probably as a result of three family bereavements over the last three years … two of which were my parents. Not to mention work pressures, which seem all too consuming as well.

To cut a long story short, as a result of all number of contributing factors to what seems like a midlife crisis, I have finally come out to my wife and sister (who else need know?). It's a difficult road to visualise from here on. I would love the friendship and support of gay men in my situation, but am frightened of the future. How to live the rest of my life authentically without destroying my family?

Suffering from 'moderate depression' recently and on SSRIs (selective serotonin reuptake inhibitors – it's a generic term for a family of antidepressants like Prozac and Citalopram, etc.) from the doctor. Can't stand being down and never allowed it to happen before, so feel out of control and unhinged compared to my usual upbeat self, but I guess it's a case of attrition for everything over the recent years.

Not in a loveless marriage, but definitely there are issues that need addressing to give us both a chance to communicate better, with more love and respect than of late. I ain't broke, but I'm badly bent! You gotta laugh or you'd cry!

After years in the wilderness it's really great to have found a place to talk to other men in my situation. Praise be to the Internet! Needless to say, I have to thank my understandably worried wife for her compassion in approving of me being here, which I ultimately hope will benefit us and our son, while I get my head straight.

I'm slowly trawling through the forums in search of a success story where husband, wife and family find a way to stay together. After twenty years, my life being in denial, duty and fidelity, I don't think I could live with the guilt of breaking up such a long-lasting friendship and my family at the same time, but with the years flying by ever faster, I'm wondering if I'll ever be able to live a life which is authentically me. Since coming out to my wife this summer, I've been increasingly depressed and alcohol-fuelled since, because there seems no solution. I just have an enormous feeling of guilt because I've ruined everyone's dreams. Hats off to the guys out there who have found new happiness and loving partners. It all sounds great if nobody gets hurt, but that's what's holding me back now (always has, really). How do you make up your mind about what action to take? How do you explain what you think you really might want without being insensitive? What if you don't get understanding and approval? Do I sound frightened of the future? Not really, just petrified! But, hey – one step at a time.

Down in the dumps. Wednesday 12 November 2008

Difficult to concentrate at work today, partly because I stayed up too late last night reading profiles and blogs, but also because I've shared more about this with my wife. We've had a much more conciliatory chat today, but it's difficult to see her so upset and hear her sobbing in private. She's coming to terms with the fact that things have changed and we have to work out together what the future holds, how to live as friends and raise our son. But sheesh, talk about feeling guilty! I've completely shattered her dreams and I haven't even acted upon any of my feelings yet, except to find support. If anyone can advise on the best type of counsellor we could get help from, I'm all ears.

On Cloud 9! Friday 14 November 2008

Talk about an emotional roller coaster. Truth is, although I can't exactly visualise a future that works for me yet, I have at least snapped out of my cloud of despair. So much has already begun to make sense now, and even relations with my wife have improved instantly despite the realisation that the future was going to be different from her expectations, and she is fully supportive – the permission I was seeking, her acknowledgement and acceptance. She's a very special person.

Anyway, one day at a time. We are still looking for suitable counselling. Looking forward to meeting more of you soon. My wife actually joked this morning: 'So you have a man in every town!' and we both laughed.

Shedding the Guilt. Thursday 20 November 2008

Remarkably, everything seems to be fitting together like a jigsaw and I wanted to share my thoughts in the hope that they will be helpful.

Although my wife and I have been best friends from the start, things had been going steadily downhill for us in one aspect of our lives, namely love and passion (no surprise there), but when you embark on married life, for whatever pressures at the time to do so, the truth is we try to do our best and be honourable, suppressing our natural desires in order to fit in and do what is expected of us. The word 'dutiful' could be my epitaph, as I realise I have tried my whole life to be what I thought others around me wanted: a straight, hard-working, loving and successful son, happily married, and a loving husband and father. Since three of our parents became poorly and died in the last few years, I feel I have also been everyone's rock, the sole breadwinner and general supporter.

I do wonder whether the sequence of events in our lives were attempts to fix something that was missing: buying a house, getting married, starting a family, changing careers, relocating, etc. Most of these events I know were also about fitting in with the general pattern of a typical married life, and in our case each change brought us a temporary distraction, but finding that complete and mutual happiness was elusive. Coming out to my wife during an argument had as much to do with my need to be recognised as a gay man as it did with desperately finding an end to all the disagreements and fall-outs that had been increasing over the years, repeating the same old arguments. I'd always been completely faithful, but I couldn't cope with the emotional one-sidedness of the relationship, and, since I had accepted that I was gay but trapped, I eventually ended up blurting it out in the middle of one such circular disagreement. I wasn't thinking straight (no pun intended), but it did effectively cut across all of the other petty issues, and then we had to deal with that instead.

Basic human needs.

Rather than a 'counsellor' as such, my wife and I both visited a hypnotherapist/mind coach about a year ago. My wife went to unblock her motivation to start work again after being a full-time mum to our son. Just two sessions gave her the ambition to believe in herself again and to start a new business from home. My own sessions were aimed at finding personal fulfilment and tackling my drinking in the context of stresses from work and our relationship. At this time, I was no longer suppressing my gay feelings (in fact, I've been out to myself since the Internet arrived), but I was still hoping I could just ignore it until I no longer needed sex. I never revealed that to the counsellor, as I felt it largely irrelevant to my 'chosen' lifestyle situation. I don't really know if the sessions helped or not. Perhaps they set the seed for me to finally come out. Still I continued to hide behind a bottle of wine most evenings and often had feelings of rejection and abandonment from my wife, because she wanted different things and we had little emotional connection.

We learned about the technique for assessing our lives by looking at the much-publicised 'six basic human needs':

- Love or connection
- Comfort or certainty
- Variety or uncertainty
- Significance
- Growth
- Contribution

While it seems most of these could be met by the practicalities of our family lives and work, and relatively easy to change, the first on the list, in hindsight, was always lacking in our situation. Realizing that this was linked to my true sexuality was a revelation, and accepting that fact suddenly relieved me of the huge burden of guilt that I have always had – that in anticipation of not living up to others' expectations, I would automatically cause them pain or anguish or even simply inconvenience. When you have low self-esteem, as many of us do, it's easier to be a doormat for fear of the consequences of sticking up for yourself and what you want. Many of us get into relationships with dominant wives and we take on a passive role. Personally speaking, I realise that I have always, and with the best of intentions, allowed my wife to choose or veto everything – decorating, holidays, meals, table manners, how to raise our son, etc., feeling that I was doing what everyone else wanted and eventually believing that nothing I said would matter or be considered anyway. Without intending to, I created an emotional vacuum for others to occupy – mostly my wife. A life of 'sacrifice' is unsustainable, and realising this makes me feel sad for us all, but I'm now determined to make it right by being my true self and, at the risk of sounding hackneyed, by allowing my own light to shine.

Feeling appreciated.

The expectation for me to be a husband/lover rather than merely a best friend, and when it comes to romance, probably we all do a pretty good job in being considerate and buying the right things, giving compliments and emotional empathy, but there's always been something missing and we've never been truly passionate, even during the first flush of excitement after we first met. In fact, I've not been too bad at being hetero in many respects, but to try to be some sort of flattering romantic would have been disingenuous. It frustrated me that while I loved my wife for her friendship, I have never been able to call her 'Love' as I do easily and naturally with my son.

Shedding the Guilt.

During the period of our counselling, I still tried to be reassuring, driven mostly by fear and guilt, that I really wanted to live the rest of my life married to my wife and I still believed I could be enough for her, and vice versa. Realising now that I could not and never will completely fulfil my wife's needs for love and connection, I am at last released from that overwhelming feeling of guilt. Thanks to wonderful support, I have been able to talk openly as myself as a gay man and not some alias. I have connected with so many people in my situation that I don't feel anything other than normal now. I feel unblocked in my emotions. I walk with a spring in my step. I no longer feel the need to drink until I'm drunk every evening, and for the first time ever, I am optimistic that I can live a happy life as a gay man as well as be a good dad and a best friend to my wife.

Without being selfish, I am not responsible for the happiness and decisions of others through life. What we need to do is work out how we can rearrange our lives emotionally so that we can move forwards into a happier episode. What the exact practical arrangements for this will be, I haven't a clue, and no doubt we will try things out and make mistakes along the way, but at least it will be the start of an authentic life for me, and despite fears of the unknown, I'm now looking forward to it. Here's to the future!

From guilt to sadness.

Yesterday was very hard for my wife. The previous night I had met up with an old school friend who I knew was gay and struck a chord with in the past. I drove to meet him and we spent the evening chatting and catching up. It was really great just to feel normal and understood. It was my first time face-to-face and 'out' to another gay man. The next day, after months of being out to my wife, the realisation of what that meant suddenly came crashing in on her, and she felt desperate and alone, with a totally new level of anguish. Having always turned to her best friend (me) for emotional support, I am now the cause of her pain, and she couldn't be comforted, nor did she feel she had anyone else to call, except perhaps my sister – who is really *my* confidante, of course.

Our son was having a sleepover for the first time, so we seized the opportunity to make reservations for a nice meal out together, and although the afternoon had been emotional, we mustered some courage and smartened up to try to give ourselves the treat neither of us felt we deserved. Talking gently and respectfully together, we began to reminisce feel-good memories from about nine years ago when we had been out for a meal with my late parents. I suddenly felt such a wave of grief I hastened for us to leave, just holding it together long enough to get back to the car before I broke down. This sadness is now so overwhelming, I feel I'm mourning all of the losses, past and future. Our lives will never be the same and it's difficult to see how we could all ever find true happiness. I know I'm not responsible for other people's, but I can surely destroy it with my actions.

My wife has also been incredibly understanding. She even gave me her blessing to go out there and discover my sexuality, but I have absolutely no appetite for that right now. I miss being able to tell her about my feelings. I've made new friends who are more understanding and genuine than ever before, and I want to share that sense of excitement and happiness with her, but this transition is the very cause of her pain. She doesn't deserve any of this, which she never signed up for in the first place.

Right now I'm having doubts about everything again. I don't have a burning desire to be 'out to the world' any more, although I would genuinely like the love and affection of the right man. Risking destroying everything we have, just to have a chance of finding that elusive 'perfect' future for selfish me, is too much to bear. We can't go backwards, I know, but perhaps there's a way we can get through this without more hurt.

Carrie Bradshaw. Saturday 22 November 2008

So what is it we need in a relationship? Sex? Understanding? Love? Mutual respect? Somebody shoot me if I begin to sound like Carrie Bradshaw from *Sex in the City*.

I believe our marriage isn't something I want anymore, but I'm clinging on to it like a frightened rat on driftwood (the ship sank long ago), and it's not fair to anyone. In fact, it will be the death of me, sooner rather than later, and that's no good for us either (except that we just doubled our life insurance this week – hmm!).

So here's a new unexpected emotion from me today. Anger. I'm having a hissy fit about being crapped on. I acquiesce to everything in the hope that it will please, I provide everything just like my dad did, and I've chosen a wife who laments never having the man I cannot be.

First Relate Session. Thursday 27 November 2008

Our first 'Relate' session was last night and it went okay, I guess. Had us both in tears, but as usual, mine were eclipsed by hers as she escalated to a new level of emotion – not her fault, just how she is, like a scared child. What's rich about it is, I've been told to be more sensitive to her feelings by not being so open about my communication online with this new support network, so as not to shove it under her nose. Even if I do so, to reassure her it's all above board and I'm not cruising for sex. So I actually have to be *more* secretive and pretend there isn't anything happening right now that might revolutionise my life. Very difficult. When I feel like I'm a new man, a whole person for once, I have to stifle it.

Moving forwards. Monday 01 December 2008

In my mind, things have reached a far more definitive state. Over the last couple of weeks in particular, I've fully come to terms with myself as being gay. I've met some great friends and become reacquainted with an old schoolmate, also a gay dad, whose friendship I value and respect greatly.

Despite the shock my wife is experiencing, having denied to herself the significance of my coming out four months ago now, I do think we'll get to a good place eventually, and my primary goal is to make the transition as painless and non-confrontational as possible. Her hopes of happiness seem to her to be shattered right now, and she's as much upset that everyone is telling her that she will have to go through all the associated bereavement emotions as she is over losing me. I take pride in the fact, however, that I'm not the abandoning type and I will be there for her in every practical way possible. It may be pie in the sky to think it, but I really hope that one day we will get through this emotional stage and become good friends again, who knows.

The Relate counsellor said it was not a good idea to work so closely together anymore, so I moved my computer from our shared office downstairs to the spare bedroom, giving us more privacy and, therefore, less tension in the air. I will occasionally sleep in here too, to get us all used to the idea that I have my own space. I am hoping that in the near future we can buy a small house or flat for me to work in – and again gradually end up spending more and more time there until it becomes more normal for our son – rather than stage a dramatic, upsetting walk-out in which he sees me 'leave' him too. It all really depends on how much my wife feels she can handle, and she may want a fresh start soon too.

I won't say I haven't felt like throwing in the towel and wanting to go back to how it all was and promise my life away to her again, but I know a juggernaut is gathering pace here and there is no going back. That, at least, is something we both agree upon for now. I am also finding alternative outcomes to wish for, when every negative worry surfaces, e.g., 'What about our son – his life will be shattered too?' type of thoughts. Actually, he will derive a very positive benefit from seeing his dad change and become happier. His life will be enriched and his understanding of gay issues will broaden, and he will also have sanctuary with me when he needs it. My wife too will have the opportunity – whether she chooses to take it or not – of finding a man who can truly and passionately love her, so she can have independence and become self-responsible and stronger.

Planning in Progress. Wednesday 17 December 2008

Having both been burning the midnight oil lately to reach a publishing deadline, we were both tired, but relieved that it was out of the way. Most of the talk between us today was initiated by her – now obviously ready to discuss future arrangements. Amazingly, and without any tears, we discussed all practical issues about things like where to live, what friends to tell, creating a gradual transition for our son, holidays, boyfriends, etc., and by the time it came to our Relate appointment, we felt we'd reached a good understanding and that actually we didn't even really need to go.

However, during the session, the subject of our past sex life reared its head for the first time, focussing on why and when it had not developed fully. Surprisingly this was not at all about my sexuality, but more on pressures which had spoiled what we did have, about acknowledging the magnitude of years of IVF treatment and parental bereavements. Initially I thought the counsellor was going to see if she could repair things, and inside my head I was screaming 'NO!'. Instead, she asked me outright if I wanted a loving partnership and sexual relationship with a man? The answer was easy: 'Yes – hopefully one day.' Good, that one was out of the way, then, but rather than focus on 'the gay thing' the discussion took an unexpected turn when she started asking about what makes us feel good about ourselves, and 'everyone's right to feel sexual, and giving yourself permission to feel good about that too'. Not only was this therapy something I'd wished I'd had twenty years ago, but it gave me bucket loads of hope and encouragement that my wife could learn to think about herself with higher regard and gain enough self-esteem to find a new partner in the future too. Herein lies another big relief, due to the fact that we've both been exposed to the impact good counselling can have, this is really becoming a positive experience at last.

Two enormous quandaries are now resolved: Firstly, I will be able to move out into my own, new 'gaydadpad' (GDP), somewhere nearby, in the spring perhaps. A new start, privacy and independence without losing family contact.

Secondly, we have acknowledged that we missed the boat long ago in terms of gaining the trust, intimacy and passion we both needed for a healthy sex life and that underplaying its importance in our marriage caused a major problem. Accepting the past and that things haven't been anyone's fault have allowed us both to realise that we could be and always were much better friends than we were lovers.

On the way home, my wife linked and squeezed my arm lovingly. It reminded me of the first time we held hands and the excitement and joy of something new and wonderful about to begin. How bizarre that this time it is the same emotions for mentally 'un-marrying' the woman I love and becoming good friends again. The tension and pressures of expectation that accompanied our marriage are starting to evaporate, and mutual respect is returning.

Monster in the Mirror? Sunday 21 December 2008

I've taken a good hard look at the past relationship with my wife since counselling started, especially about what is duty/responsibility compared to what is love/attraction, and I'm sort of amazed, perhaps even a little frightened of what I'm becoming. Not only is it the case that I'm hardening to the woman I thought I would always love, but becoming more ruthless in my mission to metamorphose into the real me at all costs, it seems. Time is short – I have an air of urgency about me and the bravado and recklessness of a seventeen-year-old. When I realise how one-sided things have been emotionally in our relationship, it now galls me that as a gentle and acquiescent man (typical gay dad, huh?) I allowed that to happen. It's myself I'm frustrated with for not being more assertive, and now that I am becoming so, it raises eyebrows around me. For once I am saying exactly what I do want (politely, of course), but the change in my script is not going down that well, particularly with my wife, who is sometimes panicked at her loss of control over me. Looking at splitting up material belongings, house and finances before moving out creates a stark illustration of just how dependent upon me she has been, and also how emotionally detached I have become so quickly. I'm not planning anything more dramatic than a gradual weaning, but it is all happening rather rapidly so far, and what I'm turning into may not be something I can look at comfortably in the mirror in the future.

Moving on. Monday 12 January 2009

Well, Christmas is out of the way and was very pleasant, albeit a little restrained and cordial. Now things are moving on again emotionally, and my wife and I made an impulse buy on a new flat near home just last week. She was amazingly courageous to instigate this, as I know she is really upset, but also wants the best for us all. I still can't believe it's happened.

It will give me a place of my own, initially to work and gradually migrate my life to as I make a new start and gain some independence, whilst keeping connected, as far as we can, as a family; a divorce wouldn't take that fact away. So we are determined to make a smooth and gentle transition for our son too.

On a personal level I am also now addressing more fundamental issues about myself and why I remained in the closet for so long. From my psychotherapist's assessment, it seems it is mostly to do with self-esteem and a pronounced social phobia. A life of pleasing others and dissipating conflict seems consistent with this.

You Got To Move It, Move It. Wednesday 04 March 2009

Moving out my office furniture to the flat was unexpectedly more emotionally significant for me. The symbolism was of being 'banished' from the house. So it feels like a sort of punishment to lose it and live in debt, and in a flat again. However, I couldn't cope with disrupting my son's or my wife's lives by forcing a sale of the family home.

Despite the plan to make the change gradual, what actually transpired was that my wife completely lost the plot soon after I moved the office to the spare room, unfortunately in front of our son. We agreed it would be best if I moved my clothes and other stuff quickly to avoid the same happening again. Thankfully our son remains oblivious to the fact that anything is really different to normal, except that he enjoys my side of the bed more often, which is cosy next to Mum. He just thinks Dad works late at the flat, which is also where Dad sleeps now, and at least two days a week I stay for dinner, put him to bed as normal and return the next day for the school run, plus other ad hoc dropping in. So far so good, but we will tell him more as soon as my wife feels strong enough to handle his questions without getting upset, not to mention being able to cope with the stigma or, worse, the pity from onlookers who find out her plight of being married to a gay man.

A Gear Change ...

Things have shifted substantially for us now, as we start adjusting to the change. What I thought would take a year or two to accomplish has now been realised in the space of around five weeks. We're left reeling a little, but I'm glad we did it. We're not looking backwards either, and on a personal level, I no longer worry so much about what other people think of me. Not to say I've shrugged off all the bad habits of the social phobia that I've become accustomed to over the years, but I don't let it bother me so much. I recognise that everyone's different, and if I get laughed at or criticised by some, I could just as easily be loved or admired by others for exactly the same things. I know I bottle things up in order to function day-to-day, but that seems okay, it works for me. It doesn't make me a heartless brute; it's just my way of coping privately without making a big song and dance.

I realise that to be gay is also NORMAL – an integral part of our society – and theories abound about why gay men were essential within a prehistoric tribe just as much as they have a role in modern society.

I realise there is no rush to 'make up for lost time' and to suddenly become promiscuous. What's right for me will be right for me, and I don't need to feel under pressure to perform like a stereotype or to change my morals just because I came out.

Coming out stages ...

Now I am also out to our close family friends, who just aren't bothered, it seems, to the point of indifference or being dismissive, which makes me really appreciate spending time with gay dads who really understand, and whom I class as better friends already. What I'm not sure about is whether our family friends will start to 'take sides': the women generally want to know why my wife isn't incensed and when she is going to start thinking about herself; the men generally don't want to discuss anything and the one who does is starting to sound uncomfortably homophobic. He says he's surprised that I'm even considering starting over and trying to find a new partner, even to the point of making a case for me to be celibate for the rest of my life, so as not to upset my family. My mother-in-law was informed while I was recently on holiday. Her reaction was surprisingly typical of most, including my wife, in that the first thing she said was 'poor Ian to have lived with this all his life and not been able to say anything'. She vowed not to treat me any differently (!?). Joking aside, I'm relieved now that at least my wife has a support network and that I don't feel it is me who has to provide all the emotional comfort, which has been nigh impossible.

Of Robert Burns, and to my wife. Monday 30 March 2009

If you feel like being maudlin and having a good weep, which is very healing, I recommend listening 'To All Who Have Lost Love', as beautifully sung by Eddi Reader of Fairground Attraction fame.

Realising Benefits. Thursday 21 May 2009

Now I'm settled in my new flat and moving on, I've noticed a good many benefits to coming out compared to when I felt closeted and trapped in the family home. I just wanted to list a few in case it helps anyone see things from a new perspective. I haven't realised all of these yet, but they boost my optimism and reinvigorate my spirits compared to how things would have been had change not been made. It's been tough at times, but in particular, I now see a better future for my wife and son too.

Confidence: I have undergone a metamorphosis of sorts since I came out. Discussing things with the counsellor, she said the only thing holding me back was myself – 'You need to give yourself permission to be happy'. Another therapist suggested I was really in fear of being 'found out', which pervaded much of my thinking and my relationships with everyone. While I've chosen only to come out to a few people, I'm not afraid to be gay anymore, and the social phobias I once had are evaporating daily as I develop a new self-worth as a normal human being – not a failed excuse for one, but a strong, independent man.

Wife self-responsible: I was always worried that my wife would become destitute and lonely if I came out and deserted her, but the fact is, she had become too reliant on me for provision of income, holidays, guaranteed emotional support, etc. As it turns out, she is now starting to think of all these issues and providing them for herself, which is giving her new confidence. I could not abandon her financially, so the security my wife had before remains intact, but a broken heart takes time to mend.

<u>Solidarity:</u> Having realised one of our couples' friendships in particular couldn't handle our new 'situation', we've actually benefited from the negativity. Their issue wasn't with me being gay so much as them not being able to cope with the change in the emotional dynamics of our relationship, and they were unfortunately quite abusive to us both in stark contrast to other friends. The result helped me and my wife unite in defiance. I'm rather pleased at the outcome, now there's more time to invest in new friendships, which we recognise are less likely to be fair-weather.

<u>Children:</u> I remain a little concerned about how my son will react to me coming out to him, which won't be until he is ready to understand. My wife is okay, ready to handle his inevitable questions now, but he is simply too young. On the positive side, he'll learn about dealing with complex emotional issues, and the importance of being true to himself and his own feelings. He'll see a dad sometimes struggling against prejudice and coping with new challenges and difficult situations. This enhanced breadth of experience is a positive thing for him growing up. All these benefits are not in spite of, but because of who I am.

August 2009

Six months into my new flat with an established routine for sharing childcare and finding my feet as an out gay man. However, old, married, monogamous habits die hard and still prevent me from thinking like a single person, but I'm developing a new network of friends and learning to think independently. All in all, I'm happier now and I'm learning how to buffer myself emotionally.

Practical issues remain to be resolved – financial being the most crucial, but my wife is now looking for a job to become more self-reliant too, and despite my ongoing commitment to my family, I will achieve more freedom once we have decided to divorce. Still not out to my son, but he's becoming more grown up every day and very well adjusted to the separation, and it's only a matter of time before we can discuss things openly.

September 2009

Now out to my son (nine) and unexpectedly have a new man in my life. We've been chatting online since July, but who'd have thought it? Meeting him in person was completely different, and we seem to have hit it off rather well. Wife is okay about it too, and we're 'happily' heading for a divorce to clear the ground so we can both move on with our lives. Guilt resurfaces periodically, but it's not a healthy emotion and something I'm at pains to rationalise away. Here's to the future!

November 2009

A year on after coming out, and now I've realised my first gay relationship and ended it after just two months. Back into the closet for me ... only kidding, never again. Unfortunately, I fell into the same old trap as others, that a gay man without children rarely understands about family commitments. Shame, really, but no regrets and time again to move on more confidently than before and to put some effort into being relaxed as me, and to getting finances and a divorce settlement back on track without external interferences. Going cold turkey on a twenty-year friendship with my wife just wasn't possible either, and I think a bereavement period has to be accounted for. What a year though!

February 2010

Eighteen months since coming out to my wife and fifteen months separated, and I am still providing for everything – very frustrating! I'm also being divorced on the grounds of my 'unreasonable behaviour' although I was always faithful, but we're finally entering some sort of financial negotiations, which I hope will make responsibilities more clear-cut. Hopefully then, my mind will be free of complications and I can start the rest of my life properly. I'm much clearer about the type of man I want in my life now, and what sort of lifestyle I want, having made some blunders over the last year. Roll on the summer when it will all be over and the sun will shine again.

March 2010

Woohoo! Divorce settlement seems to have been agreed and could all be actioned within the month. Financial independence at last, following which I could be a free man by June this year. Finally feels good to be able to start planning my future, and I can look for a proper house in earnest this spring, so that I can move on from my temporary flat. What a relief it is to get this all sorted out! Spring is looking good for other events on the calendar too, and I'm hoping to introduce the new man in my life to some people.

May 2010

Woohoo again! Found a buyer for my flat and had my offer accepted on a house in the countryside. All going really well with Mike – he's moving in with me, and my son too, and we are looking forward to tackling some big house and garden projects as soon as possible. I've had inklings of happiness levels returning to those of ten years ago and fingers crossed there are no hiccups.

July 2010

Completed on the new house, Mike (and dog) moved in too, and building work starts for the extension tomorrow. Feels wonderful to be back in a proper house and I'm full of optimism for the future. There's a grin on my face like the Cheshire Cat!

April 2011

Extension more or less completed, work ticking along nicely, home and garden improvements taking shape steadily, and loving life in the countryside and not been driven out by an angry mob brandishing flaming torches and pitchforks just yet, so times are a-changing!

Been with Mike for fourteen months now, and we're learning how to live together and navigate those early relationship hurdles … all going well so far :)

Socially we have a number of good gay friends, and we meet up regularly - much better than the fair-weather ones I had before. My son is happy too, well-adjusted although still not 'out' about me to his schoolmates – perhaps after he's been at high school for a couple of years, it might be a better time for him.

Decree absolute granted towards the end of last year, and ex-wife is selling the former marital home. Hopefully a new start will help her move on.

May 2012

Nearly two years living here with Mike. We've had some ups and downs – it's not easy learning to live with another man. Nevertheless, we've decided to tie the knot next year. This is so different from the first time around, and despite my protests about never wanting to be drawn into marriage again, I finally feel really good about life and my place in the world.

June 2013

Well, after nearly three and a half years together, Mike and I were planning to be in a civil partnership this August. Sadly, we've had to rethink what's best for us and cancel. We still care for one another, but can't commit to a lifetime together if we aren't making each other truly happy; although we've worked hard at the relationship and given it every chance, perhaps the idea of a wedding to look forward to was a bit of a sticking plaster to cover up the cracks. Perhaps taking the pressure off and just being friends again will be better for us both in the long run. It's been difficult to come to terms with my own flaws and work out what my emotions were telling me – probably too ready to accept that it was better to be with someone local than with Mr Right, and now I think I need to learn to be alone and happy in my own company a little more, instead of running away from it.

September 2013

A rather enlightening summer has passed, bearing autumn fruits rather unexpectedly in the form of a new fella in my life – Ron. Lots in common, values, interests and even seem to choose the same things off the menu in the pub!

November 2013

Hmm! Had a three-month fling. Started promisingly enough, but didn't really turn out right, so I'm going back to the drawing board, or in fact, NOT TO might be a better strategy! Trouble is that I've pretty much only known life in a relationship until now and I'm rather too good at fitting around others, except that I'm becoming less patient with other's foibles now! Perhaps I just need some time to do what I want. Either that or perhaps I just simply need another gay dad. In my limited experience they're absolutely the best in all respects and I'm unlucky enough to have never had a relationship with one!

January 2016

Well, that 'three-month fling' turned out to be a little more. A week after splitting up, and us both feeling wretched apart, ended up in Ron appearing out of the blue at the doorstep one evening to reclaim me – knight-in-shining-armour stuff! Two years later and we're still going strong and have grown closer and closer. I'm not saying it hasn't been without some wobbles, but I've realised more what I want now, and that is security and a sense of belonging. Ron and I share the same values, and he's a calming influence when I have been more emotional and impulsive at times. I think my parents would have liked him a lot. His own life has transformed too. His friends report that they've never seen him so happy.

I followed the Commons debate and the vote on equal marriage as it happened, and even though it didn't really apply to me, having no real prospects for marriage at the time, it did surprise me how much it meant to me to feel officially 'approved of' by the government. It was a big confidence boost somehow and felt like I'd been legitimised.

Ron has moved in to my house with me and my son (who lives here half the time and the other half at his mum's), since I can't contemplate moving away from the area while he is at school, but we do have a three-year plan. As soon as my son's A-levels are over, we can start looking for a house together and sell both our properties to fund it, until then, it feels great to be a settled family together, and sometime in the next year or so we're planning to get married too. No great rush, and no fanfares or cheering crowds, just us and our closest. We chose wedding rings the other week and I felt so much more relaxed and at ease with myself than I did the first time round when it was with my ex-wife. Being gay just isn't the issue it used to be, and although I still look around a little self-consciously when we're shopping at Sainsbury's together (or buying wedding rings!), most of the time I'm okay with it. Some of the self-consciousness will never really depart, I know, and I doubt we'll feel comfortable holding hands in public as I did with my wife so naturally. You can't just cast aside a lifetime of conditioning, but each year that goes by, I feel better about being gay.

I'm afraid things aren't really any better with my ex-wife though, sadly her anxiety has the better of her (it's a family trait, really), and she continues to cause problems for our son by being passive-aggressive, controlling and often irrationally angry or manically high. She's determined to remain rude towards me when she can. One Christmas Day I was made to wait outside the house for nearly half an hour after the agreed pickup time, during which they finished watching a film and not a mince pie in sight, while I shivered in the car outside. Luckily I rarely see her now. On the positive side, her hostility has helped me deal with the guilt of leaving, and I've not once looked back, aside from a few wobbles of trepidation at what the new 'gay world' might hold for me. She's never dated since we split nearly seven years ago, and someone asked me recently if she would ever get over me. I think that might explain much of her behaviour and it may be true. Perhaps her confidence is destroyed for good, and that is very sad. What a tragedy for all of us that she couldn't ever accept or understand the situation. I feel almost jealous of the dads who have managed to move on with their ex-wives' support and continued friendship.

Unfortunately, her ongoing behaviour has become more of an issue for our son, because he's going on sixteen now and doesn't want to be treated like a five-year-old anymore. He's learning to handle things by 'parenting' her outbursts as if she were a child. He knows that he always has a sanctuary with me at home, which is reassuring for him, but it's not easy at times, and I still feel guilty that I bailed out and cannot be physically there to support him.

Turning fifty last year was quite a milestone mentally and focussed my thoughts somewhat on what was realistic to hope for in the future. I suppose many of us who came out late in life can't look back without at least a little pang of regret about a wasted youth when we were physically in better shape and had our whole lives ahead of us. Although it wasn't calculated at the time, what many of us did have in compensation was the benefit of the security and love of a family life, with no direct stigma or discrimination issues to deal with around being gay in the '70s and '80s, and a lifestyle free of the risks of disease.

It's taken me thirty years to get to the same state of affairs as an openly gay man now, and I'm the most content I've ever been. Some outsiders might judge us for being cowardly or taking the easy option, but that isn't a fair reflection of what happens, nor is it without it's sacrifices.

We just do the best we can and make decisions that feel right for us at the time. Some choices don't work out, some don't feel like choices at all, but I don't have any major regrets. Life is good!

Gays in Ancient Cultures

Attitudes towards homosexuality have varied throughout history and are dependent on the culture of societies at different times and in different places. Tolerance or acceptance varies from the expectation that all males would engage in same-sex relationships, to casual assimilation or total acceptance, and whilst other societies see it as a minor sin, some repress its seemingly pervasive spread through laws, and yet others positively discriminate and prosecute against it, handing out penalties varying from custodial to death.

In *Cross-Cultural Codes on Twenty Sexual Attitudes and Practices* (1976), by Gwen J. Broude and Sarah J. Greene of Harvard University, the two collected data and compared attitudes towards, and the frequency of, homosexuality in the ethnographic studies available in the Standard Cross-Cultural Sample. This sample is made up of a number of large cultures varied enough to provide a sound basis for statistical analysis. It includes 186 different cultures, ranging from contemporary hunter-gatherers (e.g., the Mbuti – indigenous pygmy tribes of the Congo region of Africa), to early historic states like the Romans and from contemporary industrial peoples (e.g., the Russians). Broude and Greene found that out of 42 societies:

- 9 accepted or ignored homosexuality
- 5 had no concept of homosexuality
- 11 considered it undesirable, but did not set punishments
- 17 strongly disapproved and punished those that practised or promoted it

Of 70 communities, homosexuality was reported to be absent or rare in frequency in 41 of them, and present or not uncommon in 29.

It is well documented from art and literature of the time that homosexuality was frequently practiced in ancient Greece, but in later cultures influenced by Abrahamic religions, the law and the church outlawed sodomy as a crime against God and nature.

What is it that determines one society's acceptance of, and another's abhorrence to, homosexuality? Is it simply belief systems, or might there be other factors involved? Could it be that society itself can establish and/or determine sexuality and not merely create the right conditions for it to be acceptable or not within their community? When 41 communities out of 70 (58%) reported the total absence or certainly 'rarity' of homosexuality, is that because it quite literally doesn't exist in those communities?

In her introduction to *What Accounts for Cross-Cultural Variation in the Expression of Homosexuality?* Rebecca Kyle says that 'Humans are not, and perhaps have never been, passive players in their sexuality and reproduction. According to Marvin Harris (1987), "Much evidence indicates that human reproductive patterns are seldom completely at the mercy of sexual and environmental imperatives and that preindustrial population rates reflect some form of optimization effort engaged in by individuals and groups, rather than a culturally unregulated surrender to sex, hunger, and death". It is thus a fair assumption,' Kyle continues, 'that all cultures have mechanisms for controlling reproduction and fertility, whether the aim is to increase, maintain, or reduce their population. How rigid and proscriptive these mechanisms are, depends heavily on a people's mode of production (how they sustain themselves) and the perceived and actual population pressures (the factors that limit the number of people able to survive within a particular environment). Methods of controlling fertility rates include infanticide, contraceptives, post-pregnancy sex taboos, extended periods of breastfeeding, abortion, coitus interruptus and deferring marriage. Fertility rates can also be affected by tolerance or encouragement of non-reproductive expressions of sexuality including masturbation, non-coital sex, and homosexuality. It is true that attitudes towards homosexuality in particular, vary greatly cross-culturally and there is no single causal element that can account for this variation. However, population pressure can play a key role in whether or not homosexuality is practiced in a given culture.'

There are innumerable historical figures who have been labelled gay or at least bisexual, but some scholars have regarded such labelling as putting the social constraints of our own society and times upon peoples and cultures we know little about, and to whom our own notions of sexuality would be entirely alien to them and their times. A common misconceived argument is that 'no one in antiquity or in the Middle Ages experienced homosexuality as an exclusive, permanent, or defining mode of sexuality'. This claim has been countered by many examples evidenced from the ancient world, but from our modern standpoints, these occurrences of 'homosexuality' in literature and art still have to be viewed cautiously as 'gay' in the sense that we would understand it to mean.

Ancient Egypt

In ancient Egypt, there are famous tomb paintings of two high officials, Nyankh-Khnum and Khnum-hotep, who are portrayed embracing and touching nose-to-nose. Both men had families of their own, but when they died, their families apparently decided to bury them together in one tomb. There is plenty of room for speculation about the exact meaning and interpretation of the paintings, of course, but in Ancient Egypt this depiction of close nose-to-nose touching represented a kiss. Still historians and Egyptologists disagree on what it means and what was meant by showing this intimate moment between these two men. Some say it shows a clear example of homosexuality between two married men and therefore making the relationship accepted in their society. Others say that they were twins, possibly even conjoined twins, and that the paintings are showing their closeness to one another in body and spirit.

There is another well-known documented story about Pharaoh Pepi II, who frequently left his palace at night to spend hours visiting a loyal general, Sasenet. In the text from which this story comes there is one phrase which has sparked the debate about the king's sexuality: 'his majesty went into Sasenet's house and did to him what his majesty desired'. This is a common form of textural embellishment to describe sex. For this reason, some scholars are convinced that the papyrus reveals King Pepi's homosexual interests and his sexual relationship with Sasenet. Others disagree, saying that the phrase is merely alluding to Egyptian religious texts in which the sun god Râ visits Osiris in the underworld during the middle of the night. Thus, Pepi is presented in the role of Râ, using his power as the king, and Sasenet, the subordinate role of Osiris. Osiris is also a God, so perhaps this is a story about a power struggle rather than a sexual liaison. The phrase 'doing what one desires' might therefore be overrated and misinterpreted.

It remains unclear what the Ancient Egyptians' exact view of homosexuality was. Male rape, however, was clearly portrayed in their religious texts. An example of this is in the story of the rape of the God Horus by the dark God Seth, who forces himself upon his young and popular nephew in a jealous rage. Coaxing Horus into his bed after a drunken party, he tries to force himself on him, only to be tricked by the young God, as Horus catches Seth's semen in his hand and discards it later. Again, this story is about power and control, and the mystical properties of semen the Egyptians and many other ancient cultures believed in. By forcibly implanting the God's seed, Seth is trying to take control of the throne. If homosexuality was not an aspect of ancient Egyptian life, it seems odd to understand why they would have written about it in their religious texts. The moral of the story might be that the rape of young men does not humiliate them, that in the end Horus wins and the perpetrator, Seth, does not gain the power he seeks in the throne. It is nevertheless a story woven around the brutalised act of gay sex.

Further ancient Egyptian documents and literature that contain sexual-orientated stories, however, never name the precise nature of the sexual deeds. While the stories about Seth and his sexual prevalence may reveal negative views, the tomb inscription of Nyankh-khnum and Khnum-hotep suggests otherwise, that homosexuality was recognised and accepted. Nowhere is it mentioned that homosexual acts were punishable (though the death penalty for tomb-robbing was impalement. A particularly nasty end that also condemned the spirit, or Ka, to never leave the place of execution).

Ancient Greece

The earliest Western documents in the form of literary works and art objects concerning same-sex relationships between men are derived from ancient Greece. They depict homosexuality in a society in which relationships with women and with male youths were an essential and normal part of a man's life.

The formal practice of homosexual relationships was an erotic and yet often restrained affair between a free adult male and a free adolescent, and was much valued for its teaching/mentoring role. Plato described individuals who were exclusively homosexual and praised its benefits in his early writings. In the *Symposium*, he equates the acceptance of homosexuality with democracy and its suppression with despotism, saying that homosexuality 'is shameful to barbarians because of their despotic governments, just as philosophy and athletics are, since it is apparently not in the best interests of such rulers to have great ideas engendered in their subjects, or powerful friendships or physical unions, all of which love is particularly apt to produce'. Aristotle, in the *Politics*, had a different view of the barbarians, saying that 'barbarians like the Celts accorded it a special honour, while the Cretans used it to regulate the population'.

Greek men had great leeway in the expression of their sexual needs. Their wives were severely controlled and hardly even able to move about town without supervision. Men could seek adolescent boys as partners and indeed often favoured them over women. One saying went 'Women are for business; boys are for pleasure'. Though slave boys could be bought, free boys had to be courted, and documented evidence suggests that fathers had to consent to the relationship. Such relationships did not replace marriage, but concurred with it. A mature man would usually not have a mature male mate, though there were frequent exceptions, Alexander the Great, for instance. He would be the *erastes*, the lover to a younger *eromenos* or loved one. It was considered improper for the eromenos to feel desire, as that would seem to be un-masculine. The erastes, the lover and pursuer, would be driven by desire and admiration and would devote himself unselfishly to providing all the education his eromenos required to thrive in society. These relationships were emotionally as well as sexually motivated, and the Greeks believed in the power of semen as the source of knowledge, and that these relationships served to pass wisdom on.

Romans

The mentality of the Roman male psyche to 'conquer' shaped even his view on homosexual practices. As long as the man partook in the dominant, penetrative role, it was socially acceptable and considered natural for him to have same-sex relations. There was no loss to his masculinity or his social standing. Roman male liberty was defined in part with the right to preserve the body image and to keep his body from physical use by others. For the male citizen to be submissive for the giving of pleasure was seen as subservient. However, sex between men of equal status was not socially acceptable and was even severely punished in some circumstances. For instance, sex with young Roman boys was a crime, but with slaves, prostitutes, actors or anyone else of no social standing it was perfectly legitimate for the dominant Roman male.

Categorising homosexuality, as we do today, as something exclusively practised amongst one group of individuals was not a concept the Romans would have understood. Their lines of what was considered acceptable behaviour were drawn with the idea of power and domination in mind. A male who performed oral sex on another man or was the submissive partner in the sex act would have been derided and scorned and thought of as effeminate. Until the Roman Empire came under the influence of Christianity, there is only limited evidence of legal court cases against Romans who we would consider as 'homosexual' in the modern sense.

Native Americans

Before the late twentieth century, the generic term *berdache* (derived from the Persian barda meaning 'captive' or 'slave', and later in French *bardache* meaning 'male prostitute') was used to describe a mixed gender individual indigenous of the Native North American tribes. Because of its negative connotations, the more favoured term Two-spirit has replaced it.

The first Spanish Conquistadors were horrified to discover homosexuality openly practiced among the natives and attempted to crush it by subjecting them to severe punishments, including public execution by burning or being torn to pieces by dogs.

The Spanish lieutenant and later governor Pedro Fages was commander of an expedition in 1769 to explore the lands of what is now California, and wrote accounts in his diaries giving descriptive details about the natives, and reported the profusion of homosexuality. He wrote 'I have submitted substantial evidence that those Indian men who, both here and farther inland, are observed in the dress, clothing and character of women – there being two or three such in each village – pass as sodomites by profession ... They are called *joyas*, and are held in great esteem'. Joyas is Spanish for 'jewels'.

According to gay activist Will Roscoe, the presence of male-bodied Two-spirits was 'a fundamental institution among most tribal peoples'. Two-spirits were recognized in their early life development and their parents were given the choice of which path the child should follow. These were revered individuals, commonly shamans, but with powers beyond those of the ordinary shamans. Their sexual life was with the ordinary tribe members of the same sex.

Homosexual and transgender individuals were also common among other civilizations of South America, including the Aztecs, Mayans, Quechuas, Zapotecs and the Tupinamba of Brazil.

Imperial China

China and Japan shared a tradition of homosexuality that was present in their cultures until relatively recent in the two countries histories. It wasn't until about the time they came into contact with the Western world that attitudes changed. Especially in China, where only as recently as 1997 was consensual adult and non-commercial (i.e., porn) same sex made legal and the legislative penal code revised.

It wasn't until 2001 that homosexuality was removed from the Ministry of Health's list of mental illnesses, and the public health campaign against HIV/AIDS now includes education for sexually active gay men. Officially, overt police action against gay people is restricted to those engaging in gay sex acts in public places, which is also illegal for heterosexuals or gay prostitutes. But despite these recent changes, no laws exist to address discrimination or harassment on the basis of sexual orientation, and there is still media censorship of positive depictions of gay couples in films and television programmes. Gay couples are not permitted to adopt children and do not have the same privileges as heterosexual married couples.

Contact from the West started to influence Chinese society during the Qing Dynasty (1644–1912) and in Japan this was between the Edo period (1603–1868) and the Meiji period (1868–1912).

By the time of the Qing dynasty in China, there was an open acceptance that aristocrats would take male partners as well as having a wife or wives, (it was a sign of wealth and status to have more than one wife). All upper-class men were expected to marry and father children to carry on the family line, but wives, especially in the harems of the Chinese emperors, were expected only to fulfil their duties to their husband by keeping him company and rearing his children. Women who were not favourites could lead very lonely lives in the harem, while men enjoyed the freedom to bed whomsoever they pleased.

In Chinese Confucianism, primarily a social and political philosophy, little is made of sexuality, whether homosexual or heterosexual. However, the ideology does emphasize male friendships. Taoism regarded heterosexual sex without ejaculation as a way of maintaining a male's 'life essence', while homosexual intercourse was seen as something 'neutral', because the act had no detrimental or beneficial effect on his life essence.

A Tang Dynasty manuscript, 'Poetical Essay on the Supreme Joy', is a good example of the allusive nature of Chinese writing on sexuality. It sought to present 'supreme joy' (sex), in every form known to the author. The chapter on homosexuality comes between chapters on sex in Buddhist monasteries and sex between peasants. It is the earliest surviving manuscript to mention homosexuality, but it does so through phrases such as 'cut sleeves in the imperial palace' (which relates to Emperor Ai of Han (27–1 BC) who ascended the throne when he was just twenty, and the 'passion of the cut sleeve'. The story goes that after falling asleep one afternoon with his male consort, Dong

Xian, Emperor Ai cut off the sleeve to his tunic rather than disturb the sleeping Dong, when he had to get out of bed). 'Countenances of linked jade' and 'they were like Lord Long Yang', are both phrases that refer to anecdotal stories from past manuscripts. None of these expressions, however, would be recognizable as speaking of sexuality of any kind to someone who was not familiar with the literal meanings.

While these illusory language conventions make explicit mentions of homosexuality rare in Chinese literature in comparison to Greek or Japanese traditions, they are given exalted status because of their comparisons to former Golden Ages and imperial favourites.

The daring seventeenth century author Li Yu combined tales of passionate love between men with brutal violence and cosmic revenge, and in China's best-known novel, *Dream of the Red Chamber*, written in 1791 by Cao Xueqin from the Qing Dynasty, male characters engage in both same-sex and opposite-sex acts.

Though there is a tradition of eroticism in Chinese literature, but most such works have been destroyed in the periodic book burnings that have been a feature of Chinese history. However, isolated manuscripts have survived. Chief among these is the anthology *Bian er chai, Cap but Pin*, or *A Lady's Pin under a Man's Cap*, a series of short stories of passion and seduction. One, 'Chronicle of a Loyal Love', involves a twenty-year-old academic chasing a fifteen-year-old student and a bevy of adolescent male valets. In another, published in the 1630s, 'Qing Xia Ji', 'Record of the Passionate Hero', the protagonist, a valiant soldier with two warrior wives, is seduced by his younger friend, an unusual situation, as stereotypically it was the older man who took the initiative.

Chinese art also has many examples of same-sex acts that have survived. Though no large statues are known to still exist, many scrolls and paintings on silk can be found in private collections that explicitly depict men having sex with other men.

Imperial Japan

In Japanese society, homosexuality developed along social hierarchal lines. In the warrior classes and especially amongst those who adhered to the bushido code of honour of the samurai, a relationship between the nenja and a wakashū, a youth in his teens, was seen as a special bond between men – a continuation of their training and a demonstration of their trust and love for one another. The relationship was mutual and voluntary and the samurai shudō was strictly role-defined; the nenja was seen as the active, desiring, penetrative partner, while the younger, sexually receptive wakashū was the submissive partner to the nenja's attentions, out of love, loyalty, and affection, rather than sexual desire. Among the samurai class, adult men were (by definition) not permitted to take on the wakashū role; only pre-adult boys (or, later, lower-class men) were considered desirable.

There are references in ancient Japanese literature to same-sex love, but these are so subtle and obscure as to be unreliable. This again is to do with the language, as terms relating to homosexuality as we know of it today simply didn't exist or apply. The Japanese term 'nanshoku' literally translates as 'male colours'. The character for 'colour' has a dual meaning of sexual pleasure both in Chinese and Japanese. Thus the term, 'male colours', was widely used in written works to denote male-to-male sex.

In Japanese culture it was commonplace for men to declare in writing their affections towards friends of the same sex. We have to bear in mind that it was only the ruling classes who were able to read and write, as was the situation in every pre-industrial society. In *The Tale of Genji*, written in the eleventh century, men are frequently moved by the beauty of youths. In one scene the hero is rejected by a female character and so instead sleeps with her younger brother. 'Genji pulled the boy down beside him ... Genji, for his part, or so one is informed, found the boy more attractive than his chilly sister.'

The Tale of Genji is a novel, but there are several Heian-era diaries that contain references to homosexual acts and 'handsome boys retained for sexual purposes' by the emperors.

Several writers have noted the strong historical tradition of open bisexuality and homosexuality among male Buddhist institutions in Japan. Nanshoku relationships inside monasteries were typically pederast: an age-structured relationship where the younger partner is not considered adult. The older partner would be a monk, priest or abbot, while the younger was an acolyte and adolescent boy. The relationship would be dissolved once the boy reached adulthood or left the monastery. Both parties were encouraged to treat the relationship seriously and to conduct the affair honourably. The nenja might even write a formal vow of their fidelity. Outside the monasteries, monks were renowned for having a particular predilection for male prostitutes, which caused much ridicule.

There was no religious opposition to homosexuality in Japan, and artists were free to depict the kami, or spirits, engaging in homosexual sex with each other. During the Tokugawa period, some of the Shinto gods were seen as guardian deities of nanshoku.

Mediaeval Europe

Mediaeval Europe heralded a period, and entire continent, that was dominated by the harshest legislation and intolerance towards homosexuality and those who practised it. It is no coincidence that this era and region was subject to widespread Christian indoctrination. By the twelfth century, but also before that, homosexuality was a vice considered punishable by death. The moral story of Sodom and Gomorrah in the Book of Genesis from the Old Testament could not have warned more severely of the sinfulness found in collective, close-quartered city living, and those that might think to stray from the path of righteousness in the crowded, anonymous alleyways and streets – a stark illustration of what would befall innocent peasants who migrated to the cities for work and a 'better' living.

State persecution of homosexuals reached its zenith during the Inquisition, though it is unlikely that homosexuality itself would have been cause enough for someone to be tried, but rather their stance and opposition against the Church because of it.

The **Cathars**, Gnostic Christians whose beliefs and practices dated from the earliest Christian times that predated the Catholic Church, were accused of Satanism and sodomy, and in 1307, accusations of sodomy and homosexuality were levelled during the **trials of the Knights Templar**.

There are prominent figures from the time about whom there is evidence of them conducting homosexual relationships including, Edward II, Richard the Lionheart and William Rufus, and historian Allan A. Tulchin says that a form of male same-sex 'marriage' existed in Mediaeval France and possibly in other areas of Europe as well. This was something called 'enbrotherment', which the Romans invented, that allowed two men to share living quarters, pool their resources, and effectively live as a married couple. They would share 'one bread, one wine, one purse,' and this persisted into Mediaeval times.

It was around 400 AD that Christianity began to introduce a new sexual code that focused on the religious concepts of holiness and purity. The Church, which was gaining social and political power by the middle of the third century, originally had two approaches to sexuality. One was much like their Greco-Roman predecessors, whereby they did not view or judge any sexuality, instead only judged the act itself. The second, and predominantly held approach within Christian society, was an entirely opposed view. Sex was only for procreation purposes, and therefore the Church promoted a sex life focused on platonic, pure and God-fearing, man-woman relationships. Sexual activity for any other purpose, oral, anal or masturbation, including heterosexual sex acts, other than sex for creating life, was considered and widely accepted as sinful.

Punishments for homosexual behaviour became ever harsher, and by the thirteenth century, male homosexual acts in some countries resulted in castration on the first offense, dismemberment on the second, and burning on the third.

Artists cannily managed to disguise depictions of admiration for the male form in their paintings by using religious themes as content, and there was a significant rise in the late Mediaeval period of such artworks when Latin and Greek art was revitalised in Europe. During this period of the **Renaissance**, 1300–1700, wealthy Italian cities, such as Florence and Venice, attracted artists of all kinds and were renowned for their promiscuous proliferation of same-sex love, but even while many of the male population were engaging in homosexuality, the authorities were busy prosecuting, fining, and imprisoning them, and by the mid-fourteenth century many cities in Italy had laws that could enforce confiscation of an offender's property for just being homosexual.

This is John's Story

I am a sixty-year-old guy, divorced with four adult children and living in Essex. I can remember right back to primary school not understanding why all the other boys got excited by female breasts, which did nothing for me. I used to enjoy tickling other boys in the genitals whilst play fighting, but never really thought anything of it. Secondary school was awkward, as I was very shy and naive and young for my age. However, physically I developed early and got aroused very easily in the changing rooms, which was highly embarrassing. Again I had no idea what being gay was all about and did not recognise what my body was telling me. In my youth it was unheard of to be gay, the only reference I can remember was of old men in raincoats. My parents would not have approved at all, so I suppose I just buried it deep within me. I can remember running around in the sun naked on some heath land in my early teens with some lads a bit younger than me for a dare, and I distinctly remember telling myself afterwards never to do that again, as I felt I might be disgraced by my actions.

If I look back, I struggled with life, as I was so shy and lacked confidence. I think a lot of that was due to not understanding where I fitted in. If only I knew then what I know now. I met a girl whilst I was at work, introduced to me by a friend, and at the age of twenty-three I was married. She was three years younger than me and it was the first relationship for both of us. Neither of us had had any sexual experience, so it seemed good at the time, and although I never really had a strong desire to have children, I was persuaded that it was normal, so we did. Four great kids in total, now ranging from nineteen to thirty-two. I have really enjoyed bringing them up. Our first child had seizures at five months, and this left her with severe learning difficulties and needing twenty-four--hour care. We managed with very little help for seventeen years, but my wife and I rowed constantly with the pressure, whilst the outside world thought we made a great couple. I began to realise how unhappy I was and also how unhappy I seemed to make my wife. She told me she still loved me, but a few months later I mentioned in passing to my female GP how bad things were at home and she bluntly told me to leave. I was totally shocked, as I had no idea she had realised how awful things had got.

  I left home three months later after a particularly bad row, to live with my eighty-four--year-old father, who was recently widowed after fifty years. I seemed to have swapped one caring role for another, but we made a family deal where I kept an eye on him and he provided a roof over my head, which in turn kept my family in their home. I went to a great counsellor every two or three weeks; she knew all my history and was absolutely brilliant at keeping me going. I got rid of all my angst in my sessions with her. I told our female GP I liked men, but she just dismissed it with a comment along the lines of that she still didn't think that was the main reason why I left.

My dad eventually went into care, with severe dementia, and for a while I carried on living in his house. My ex remarried to an acquaintance of ours, who moved in one month after meeting her, which was a shock, but very helpful financially. They married the following summer just ten days after we divorced, but I had to pay their mortgage for a further seven months whilst I tried, unsuccessfully, to get some security of tenure for my disabled daughter, who lives in a flat in part of the house. (They bought me out and I gave away two thirds of our joint assets, but did keep my pension.)

After many years, I get on fine with my ex-wife now (very difficult and acrimonious for several years, though), and as we have a wedding of our daughter coming up, it's very pleasing to think we can both enjoy being on the top table without any difficulty. My family initially pushed us this way, without asking me, by including me and my ex-wife and her then boyfriend (now husband), and my children, to all family events. This was hugely difficult for me for a long while and I did resent it at the time, but they knew how they wanted things to end up and it's been a good result for all, especially the children, who are all grown up and are very happy that we can all socialise together.

I came out to my children when they were seventeen, fourteen and eleven. My eldest has no speech, so it's difficult to work out what she understands or not. She is quite knowing, so I feel she has worked things out for herself. I got outed via my son and my wife's boyfriend about eighteen months after I left the family home. My ex and her boyfriend put the things my son had said, in all innocence, together and did a bit of digging about my then boyfriend, and found out that his wife had outed him as gay, which in turn then outed me. My wife then told all my family and I assume most of our friends before phoning me three weeks later in the middle of a working day and challenging me. I'm no good at lying, and when I asked her who she had told, she only admitted to me that she had told my sister and brother, though I guessed everyone else now knew, which made me realise I needed to tell the children very quickly to avoid them hearing it from another source.

I called them into my office around 4pm after school, and my seventeen-year-old ran screaming, hysterically, out of the office. The others said they all loved me and I was the same person I had always been, and by 7pm my daughter called me to say could she still have her driving lessons! My fourteen-year-old walked out of my office, sobbing, saying things would never be the same, but she too got used to the idea over time, though she is much quieter and reserved. I told our son on holiday when he was eleven and he hasn't been fazed much since. None of them have 'celebrated having a gay dad' like I hear some do, but I have excellent relationships with all of them, and they have all picked lovely partners and seem to be very happy in their relationships, which is very pleasing.

I bought my own house a few years ago and am very lucky to have a nice home, a good job and kids that accept me as a gay dad. So I moved into a lovely house by the river just fifteen minutes' walk from my office. I live there on my own now, finding that having young gay lodgers was just too much of a challenge. As the years have gone by, it's quite accepted by everyone now that I am gay. When I recently celebrated my big sixtieth birthday, my cousins, whom I rarely see, said, 'Oh we worked that out years ago,' as did my aunt, who at eighty-six was completely unfazed by it despite her strong religious beliefs.

As I run my own business, I get put in situations every now and again where I am at dinner with a client and they say, 'You have been on your own for a while now, have you found a girlfriend yet?' I just reply, 'Well, it's a boyfriend I'm looking for these days,' and so far, I have had only positive responses. I very much took the wind out of one very wealthy client whom I suspect wanted to have a bit of fun with me as he had guessed my sexuality, then didn't know what to talk to me about after I just outed myself to him straight away.

I am involved with the local community and sing in a local church choir. I am chairman of Outhouse East, our local LGBT charity, and I belong to the Gay Classic Car Group, which has topped its 1,000th member. I have three classic cars, which I enjoy taking to lots of the GCCG events. I also belong to the Gay Outdoor Club, although I don't actually make many of their walks. I enjoy my home, when I am there, and my garden. I also enjoy going to as many of the GADS's events I can fit in.

I have had two gay relationships, but my first partner stayed with his wife and they have recently retired together, as that's what she wanted, and I wasn't going to be the third person in that relationship. I am still good friends with both of them. Boyfriend number two wasn't really out, which made things difficult. He was a lovely chap, who came out partially when going out with me, but I felt that it wasn't going to last, and he later decided to go back in the closet. Until a while later he met Mr Right and came out to everyone, got civil-partnered and emigrated to the USA. Shows what the right connection with a partner can do to your life. I am still looking for my very own Mr Right, which gets harder as you get older, and I get more used to living on my own. However, I know there has to be that mutual spark, and I won't compromise after so many years of unhappy marriage in the wrong relationship.

    I don't miss an invite out, I find I am working harder than ever, and I do enjoy the challenge. As I get older, I find gut feelings are so much stronger, and I let them guide me to better decisions. I also believe balance is the most important part of enjoying my life.

Gay slang

Gay slang is not a modern phenomenon. In the eighteenth-century molly-house subculture of London, gay slang was prolific as a modification of thieves' speak and the slang used by prostitutes. 'Molly-houses' was a term used to describe meeting places for homosexual men in eighteenth- and nineteenth-century London. These were taverns, coffee shops or even private rooms where men would meet, socialise and pick up male prostitutes.

Gay slang was also part of homosexual subcultures in sixteenth-century Italy and seventeenth-century Portugal, Spain, and France. In the 1730s, Dutch homosexuals talked to each other in what they called 'John girlish', and in ancient Greece, the debauched and apparently 'effeminate' priests of the Thracian Goddess of immodesty and desire, Cotytto, worshipped at night in lewd nocturnal rites and had their own obscene language.

In the 1950s, a jury in Britain presiding over a homosexual trial had to be provided with a glossary of 'queer' terms to enable them to understand the testimony of the witnesses.

The bulk of gay slang originates from within the homosexual community itself and is used by homosexuals for the benefit of their own cultural solidarity and not, as some might think, as a means to cope with or undermine the counterpart straight culture. It was not used as a means to convey secret messages either. Although Polari, a discrete gay lingo which was popularly used amongst the homosexual community of London in the 1960s, enabled men to talk freely about the attractiveness of another man's 'basket', for example, without him knowing. But the origin of some gay slang words is unknown to both homosexual and heterosexual academics and therefore undermines any argument that homosexual culture is determined by the structures and labels imposed upon it by mainstream 'straight' society. For example, 'xia zhuan', i.e., 'intimacy with a brick', is slang for homosexuality in Japanese and has an unknown origin. Similarly, the origin of 'faggot' is unknown. It first appeared in America in 1914 when 'fagots', i.e., 'sissies', were described as going to a 'drag ball'. A certain Reverend Fred Phelps noted 'that just as a fagot is a bundle of sticks that fuels fire, homosexuals fuel the wrath of God', but this does not explain the origin of 'faggot'.

Rictor Norton says 'that we simply don't know the origins of the most common homosexual slang words that became popular through the 1930s to the 1950s; words such as *gay, faggot, queer, fairy*. Throughout the 1920s and 1930s *faggot* was used mainly in the black culture of Harlem. It is unrelated to the British public school fag system, 'and has no connection to faggots as bundles of sticks', he says. *Faggot* probably comes from the word *baggage*, the sixteenth-century slang for 'harlot', as in the affectionate insult 'You saucy baggage!' The word *fairy* appeared in the 1870s and was universally understood for its homosexual connotations by the 1890s.

Gay meaning 'merry' or 'exuberantly joyful' can be traced back to mediaeval French *gai*, but its earlier origins are unknown. For the past two or three centuries *gay* has had sexual overtones in general. In the eighteenth century lewd behaviour was part of the 'gay life', enjoyed by both men and women. Rakes and men-about-town were called 'gay blades'. The *Dictionary of the Vulgar Tongue* published in 1811 gives 'the gaying instrument' as a slang term for the penis.

In the nineteenth century, good-time girls and streetwalkers were called 'gay ladies' and brothels were called 'gay houses'. Male hustlers plied the same streets as female prostitutes, and the word *gay* acquired a homosexual connotation. One of the male prostitutes rounded up during the Cleveland Street scandal of 1889 described himself in court as 'gay'. In London, Rev. John Church, a minister who performed marriages between men at a homosexual brothel in Vere Street in 1810, was described in a pamphlet of 1813 as 'the *gay* parson': the word *gay* was italicized, obviously to call attention to it.

Though there is little evidence, homosexual connotations of the word *gay* go back even further. For example, in Mary Pix's play *The Adventures in Madrid*, which was performed in 1706, a girl character dressed as a boy is pursued by a man named 'Gaylove' who calls her his little 'Ganymede' and 'fairy'. Surely this means what it seems to mean?

We can say without doubt that *gay* was used in the 1930s in Midwest America as slang for 'homosexual'. In a *Dictionary of Underworld Slang* published in 1933, a *gay cat* was defined as 'a homosexual boy'. It was prison slang for the younger man who serviced older partners. Jack London in *The Road* published in 1907 said a gay cat was an apprentice hobo. In the American hobo subculture of the 1920s and '30s, it was common for older and younger tramps to pair up. The young hobo would keep a lookout while the older man did some pilfering. It's not hard to see how *gay cat* became slang for a punk who offered sex in return for money or a treat or protection.

The upper classes became familiar with the term by the late 1930s, probably while 'slumming it' in the underworld, or perhaps through artistic bohemian circles. Some early movies even used the word 'gay' as a coded reference. In the 1938 comedy *Bringing Up Baby*, when Cary Grant is asked why he's wearing a frilly nightgown, he replies, 'I just went gay all of a sudden.' Apparently this line wasn't scripted, but was ad-libbed by Grant. Some argue that this code word was used in even earlier movies.

The word *queer* was used by gay men about a decade earlier than *gay*, and it similarly has a centuries-long non-gay history, meaning odd, eccentric, disreputable or bent. It was the most commonly used term, together with *fairy*, before World War II. It was used mainly by 'ordinary' and 'straight-acting' gay men in preference to a host of effeminate words such as nellie queens, margeries, fairies, pansies, nancy-boys.

By the 1940s the homosexual meaning of *gay* was common knowledge to those in the American gay subculture and it became common in Britain by the 1950s. From the late 1950s it was increasingly extended to cover women as well as men. There were organisations for 'gay men and women' and for a short period, from about 1965 to 1973, lesbian activists employed it, but they began rejecting it as the gay liberation movement began fragmenting into ever-purer ideological camps.

Crucial to the gay explosion was the adoption of slogans such as 'Gay Power', 'Gay is Good' and 'Gay Pride'. GAY was perfect as a short, powerful, arresting image and became a potent word for organisations, leaflets, newspapers, magazines and T-shirts. London's *Gay News* was born in 1972.

Gay slang words don't construct identities. They can widen or narrow the possibilities for expression, but it would be a mistake to assume that identity didn't exist prior to the words currently used to describe that identity. For example, plenty of words were used to identify different types of gay men in England in the eighteenth century: molly, endorser, Gany-boy, madge cull, mameluke, margery, patapouf, queen and aunt. These words were in addition to older terms such as catamite, sodomite and buggerer. Terms like 'unnaturalist' or 'invert' (which were both used in the eighteenth century) and 'homosexual' (coined in 1868) were eventually taken up by the modern medical establishment, but they had no impact on the working-class subcultures where most gay slang is employed.'

List of current gay slang words and terminology

Bareback: to have anal sex without the protection of a condom and usually meaning to ejaculate inside the anal passage but can also mean to withdraw at or prior to ejaculation.

Bear: a hairy chested and bearded, heavy-set and often muscular man who projects a rugged 'cliched' image of masculinity. A large belly is a defining characteristic. The image is of the dominant male often dressing in biker gear or lumberjack style clothing. The outdoors and manliness prevail.

There are several sub-cultures of bears:

- Muscle Bears: Bears whose size comes from muscle and not from fat
- Polar Bears: Older bears with grey or white facial and body hair
- Sugar Bears: Effeminate bears often shunned by more masculine bears

Bi: sexually attracted to both men and women

Bi-curious: people who show some interest or curiosity for sexual activity with a person of the same sex, but who distinguish themselves from the 'bisexual' label. It implies that the individual has either no or limited homosexual experience and until they do so, remain simply 'curious' as to what it's like.

BJ: 'Blow-job' sucking on a penis usually to the point of its ejaculation.

Boi: a young man who prefers older partners and is the 'boi' in a 'daddy-boi' relationship. It enables the younger partner to differentiate themselves from a 'boy' who might be someone underage. Some males call themselves a 'boi' well beyond their 20's, and especially so if they seek to be with older men. Often, though not always, a 'boi' is the submissive role.

Bottom: the guy being penetrated by a 'Top' through anal sex, often called the passive or submissive role.

Breed/breeding: to ejaculate inside another's anal passage.

Buggery: is very close in meaning to sodomy and first appeared in the Buggery Act of 1533. It is the act of anal intercourse committed with man or animal.

Bukkake: is the noun form of the Japanese verb bukkakeru, to splash with water, but in the sexual context and now widespread through its use in porn, bukkake means to ejaculate on another's face and usually two or more men doing the ejaculating.

Butt plug: a sex-toy to stimulate the prostate. Basically a cone shaped plug that is pushed into the rectum and held in place with a flared flat-shaped end that prevents it from travelling up the bowel.

Cock-ring: the purpose of a cock-ring is to maintain the rigidity of an erect penis by cutting off the flow of blood back from the penis. It does not stop ejaculation, but can prolong it. It can be worn when the penis is flaccid to make it more pronounced and give a bigger bulge. If choosing a metal one, make sure it is not too tight as it has been known for metal rings to go on when the penis is soft but impossible to get off when hard, and because the blood is trapped, it is harder for the erect penis to deflate. This can cause serious medical issues. Though a lot comes down to aesthetic choice, leather or material ones that fasten with Velcro or buttons are less likely to cause problems. A cock-ring shouldn't be worn for more than 30 minutes and certainly should be taken off before sleep. A triple cock ring or triple crown, is a cock ring which has additional rings for restraining the testicles. During orgasm the testicles usually retract towards the body before ejaculation. A triple crown changes and intensifies the sensation of orgasm by forcing the testicles to stay away from the body.

Cottage/cottaging: Originally, English park toilets which resemble little cottages hidden amongst the trees and other such places, where men go with the intention of having sex with other men. The term is now widely used for any public toilet, i.e. in shopping centres, airports, cinemas etc., where men can meet for sex. The term has been in use since Victorian times. Cottaging is the act of anonymous sex in public lavatories.

Cruising: hanging out in public places, i.e. toilets, saunas, woods, anywhere that might be frequented by other men looking for casual, anonymous sex. Usually these places are well known in the gay community and often the general public can be completely innocent of what is going on.

Cub: a more youthful version of a 'bear'. Usually smaller framed and typically refers to the passive partner in a 'bear' relationship. A cub's beard is usually clipped shorter and his image might be less rugged, more tailored than his counterpart 'bear'. Cub sub-groups include:

- Muscle Cubs: Body size is attributable to muscular composition, not body fat
- Sugar Cubs: Effeminate cubs

Daddy: an older man sexually involved with or has a sexual interest in younger men. The age gap may vary, but the relationship mimics something of a parental, father-son dynamic. The 'daddy' will provide emotional support as well as sexual dominance in the relationship. A Daddy is completely different from a 'sugar daddy', it has nothing to do with financial status or wealth.

Daisy-chain: a sexual position involving multiple partners. One is sucking another's penis, the second is pleasuring a third, and so on. This can be by mutual masturbation as well.

Dildo: sex toys, usually in the shape of penises for inserting into the anus. They come in different sizes, colours, vibrate or not.

Facial: ejaculating onto the face and/or into the mouth of a partner.

Felching: the sexual practice of sucking one's own semen out of the anus of a partner after having ejaculated. This semen can then be passed into the mouth of the partner from whom it has just been sucked.

Fisting: the sex act which involves inserting a hand into the rectum and thought to be the only sexual activity 'invented' in the twentieth century. Once insertion is complete, the fingers are either clenched into a fist or kept straight. Fisting may be performed solo or, more commonly, with a partner. Putting anything into the rectum runs the risk of tearing the inside and possible infection.

Fleshlight: is the number one selling brand of sex toy marketed to men as an aid to masturbation. It was designed by Steve Shubin who patented his invention in 1998 as a 'device for discreet sperm collection'. The name was coined from the flesh-like material used in the inner sleeve and the plastic outer casing which resembles a flashlight or torch. The inner sleeve, which comes in various designs: mouth, vagina or anus, is made from medical grade phthalate-free polymers. The company who manufacture Fleshlights, Interactive Life Forms, calls the material 'Real Feel Superskin'. Despite the interior sleeve's similar texture and appearance, it is not made from silicone, latex or plastic, and the exact formula is a closely guarded secret under the patent.

Freeballing: like going 'commando', freeballing is going without underwear, but more public and exhibitionist where trackie bottoms or shorts are worn so that the bulge, testicles and penis are visible freely moving under the material.

Glory hole: a hole in a wall or partition, purposefully created for the act of sexual encounters and most popularly fashioned between public toilet cubicles by the guys who cruise there. The glory hole is perhaps the ultimate in anonymous sex, where no contact in the encounter takes place other than between the mouth, penis, hand and sometimes anus. Adult video booths and gay saunas often have 'ready-made' glory holes.

Gym bunny: a guy who spends an obsessive amount of time in the gym working on sculpting his body, not for health reasons, but so that he can show off at a club or on the beach.

Hookup: a date, usually, but not exclusively, arranged online, casual and with less of the confinements and expectations of a proper 'date'.

Jock: a sports loving man who enjoys keeping fit and healthy and looking after his body.

Muscle Mary: see gym bunny, but muscle Mary's are often more camp.

NSA: No strings attached, i.e. casual sex.

NSF: Non-scene fun. On dating or hook-up websites this would indicate someone who doesn't hang out on the gay scene, often married, bi-sexual or in a relationship and are just looking for someone to 'play' with.

Otter: a slim and less hairy man than a 'bear' and perceived as more 'playful' and less 'aggressive' than a 'wolf'. The otter's beard would be well groomed and possibly no more than clipped stubble. He still sports chest and pubic hair. His body type is lean and naturally healthy and athletic.

Lube: short for lubricant. Water based gels are the most widely used in aiding smoother sex and reducing friction.

POZ: HIV positive.

Rimming: the act of licking, kissing, sucking and often inserting the tongue into a partners' anus. For obvious health reasons, make sure the person being rimmed is very clean before putting your mouth or tongue anywhere near their anus.

Scat: or Coprophilia (from the Greek kopros – excrement, and philia – liking or fondness), also called scatophilia or scat (from the Greek skata – shit). It is the sexual arousal and pleasure from the feel, touch, sight and smell of faeces. Scat play can involve acts such as smearing faeces on the body, defecating on a person's body, watching a person defecate, or even eating faeces. While many people find this fetish repulsive, those that are drawn to it do so because of the smooth, warm feeling of faeces as well as the taboo surrounding it. Studies have shown that this fetish is not exclusive to either homosexuals or heterosexuals, and although this is a minority fetish, the interest in it in both communities is about equal. A word of warning: for obvious reasons the implications of engaging in this fetish come with serious health risks.

Smooth: or smoothie, is someone who keeps their body, (usually chest, armpits and genitals), shaved or waxed clean of hair.

Snowballing: Snowballing or snow-dropping, is the practice of taking someone's semen into the mouth and passing it back to them by kissing or dropping it into their mouths, usually several times and particularly so in a group, hence the term 'snowballing'. Researchers surveying over 1,200 gay and bisexual men at New York LGBT community events in 2004 found that around 20 per cent of them said they had engaged in snowballing at least once. Most heterosexual men are uncomfortable with the practice.

Spit-roast: a sex position involving three. The one in the middle gives oral sex while at the same time is penetrated from behind by a third.

Sub: referring to the submissive partner in a relationship (see bottom). The one who is penetrated rather than the penetrator.

Top: referring to the dominant partner in a relationship, i.e. the one to penetrate, be on 'top'.

Twink: is a term used to describe gay young men in their late teens to early twenties. They are attributed with attractiveness, have little or no body or facial hair, are slim and of average muscle build. A twink is apparently 'memorable for his outer packaging and not his inner depth'. The term twink has been recorded in use since 1963, and may be derived from an older British gay slang term twank meaning 'a homosexual prostitute, willing and ready to become any dominant man's partner'. There is an acronym that states that twink stands for, 'teenaged, white and into no kink'.

Vanilla: means plain and conventional sex and would generally apply to someone who is not willing or interested in exploring or experimenting in any sexual practice that strays from the norm.

Wolf: a slimmer version of the 'bear', with similar characteristics of sexual assertiveness, but with a cunning intellect. They are semi-hairy, muscular, lean, attractive, and have facial hair. Older wolves might be coined 'silver' or 'grey' wolves, and the connotations are that they are free spirits of the wild and slightly dangerous.

Polari

Polari is a gay slang language which has almost died out now, but was more commonly used in the 1960's when homosexuals were in need of a private, discrete way of communicating amongst themselves.

Polari featured heavily in the 'Julian and Sandy' sketches on the BBC radio programme 'Round the Horne' in the late 60's. A few words like 'bona' can still be seen in gay publications. There are even hairdressers called 'Bona Riah'.

Polari was never clearly defined, it was an ever-changing collection of slang taken from various sources including Italian, English (backwards slang, rhyming slang), circus slang, canal-speak, Yiddish and Gypsy languages. In London, there was a West End dialect, based on theatre-speak, which was posher than the East End dialect, based on canal/boat-speak.

Here are a selection of some Polari words. For more see: http://chris-d.net/polari/

- basket: the bulge of a man's genitals through clothing
- bod: body
- bona: good
- carts/cartso: penis
- carsey/khazi: toilet
- chicken: young boy
- charpering omi: policeman
- ecaf: face
- esong: nose
- fantabulosa: wonderful
- fruit: queen
- meese: plain/ugly
- naff: not available for fucking
- oglefakes: glasses
- omi: man
- omi-polone: effeminate or gay man
- palare pipe: phone
- polari: chat/talk
- polone: woman
- riah: hair
- riah shusher: hairdresser
- troll: to walk about, especially looking for trade

Helpful Links

Gay Dads UK http://gaydads.co.uk/

An active community for GayDads in the UK. Find support in the forum or chatroom. Attend events organised by members and meet gay dads in your area.

GOC http://www.goc.org.uk/

Gay Outdoor Club with 40 years' experience in helping people to try new activities and make new friends. The members club is run by the people who go on its events. Most events are free and you can just turn up without booking. Joining GOC means all of the money goes to running the club and none on salaries or profits. Visitors to the website can get a good idea of the range of activities, but only members can fully access details on the events.

Imaan http://www.imaan.org.uk/

Imaan supports LGBT Muslim people, their families and friends, to address issues of sexual orientation within Islam. It provides a safe space and support network to address issues of common concern through sharing individual experiences and institutional resources.

Imaan promotes the Islamic values of peace, social justice and tolerance through its work, and aspires to bring about a world that is free from prejudice and discrimination against all Muslims and LGBT people.

OUTeverywhere http://www.outeverywhere.com/

OUTeverywhere is a social club for gay people. Whether you're looking for gay dating or just to make more gay friends in your area and beyond, their online messaging, chat areas and photo profiles are complemented by a huge range of events.

Pink News http://www.pinknews.co.uk/home/

PinkNews is a UK-based online newspaper marketed to the lesbian, gay, bisexual and transgender community (LGBT). It was founded by Benjamin Cohen in 2005 and covers politics, religion, entertainment, finance, and community news for the LGBT community in the UK and worldwide.

Sarbat http://www.sarbat.net/

Sarbat is a social and support group for LGBT Sikhs. They offer a platform for like-minded Sikhs from all walks of life and aim to promote the LGBT Sikh cause in a fair and courteous manner.

Stonewall http://www.stonewall.org.uk/

Stonewall (officially Stonewall Equality Limited) is a lesbian, gay, bisexual and transgender (LGBT) rights charity in the UK named after the Stonewall Inn of 'Stonewall' riots fame in New York City's Greenwich Village. Now the largest LGBT rights organisation not only in the UK but in Europe, it was formed in 1989 by political activists and others lobbying against Section 28 of the Local Government Act. Its founders include Sir Ian McKellen, Lisa Power MBE and Michael Cashman CBE.

Stonewall diversified into policy development for the rights of lesbian, gay and bisexual people after Labour came to power in 1997. It remains a lobbying organisation rather than a membership organisation.

Terence Higgins Trust http://www.tht.org.uk/

Terrence Higgins Trust is a British charity that campaigns on various issues related to AIDS and HIV. In particular, the charity aims to reduce the spread of HIV and promote good sexual health (including safe sex); to provide services on a national and local level to people with, affected by, or at risk of contracting HIV; and to campaign for greater public understanding of the impact of HIV and AIDS.

UNISON https://www.unison.org.uk/about/what-we-do/fairness-equality/lgbt/

UNISON, the public service trades union, holds national conferences for its LGBT members. UNISON fights discrimination and prejudice in the workplace on behalf of its lesbian, gay, bisexual and transgender (LGBT) members. They work together with local and national groups of LGBT members to campaign and provide support for its members.

Acknowledgements

My foremost gratitude goes to the ten men who gave so much of themselves to make this book possible. Though it can be cathartic to unburden oneself of things never normally spoken about, it is no mean feat to do so. They talked about very personal and emotive issues in the hope that other gay men in similar situations would be able to relate to their stories and take something positive from them. I think they have exceeded that proposition.

A special mention goes to Charlie Condou, Alastair Appleton and Rictor Norton for their brilliant contributions, without which this book would be a less valuable one.

I must also thank Elly Donovan and Vicky Edwards at Elly Donovan PR for their support and help in getting *Gay Dad* out there.

Made in the USA
Charleston, SC
18 June 2016